When Time Stood Still

Rachel Lev-Wiesel & Ziv Koren

London | New York

Published by Clink Street Publishing 2014

Copyright © Rachel Lev-Wiesel and Ziv Koren 2014

First edition.

The author asserts the moral right under the Copyright, Designs and Patents Act 1988 to be identified as the author of this work.

All rights reserved. No part of this publication may be reproduced, stored in a retrieval system or transmitted, in any form or by any means without the prior consent of the author, nor be otherwise circulated in any form of binding or cover other than that which it is published and without a similar condition being imposed on the subsequent purchaser.

ISBN: 978-1-909477-32-2
Ebook: 978-1-909477-33-9

This book was made possible by the support of the
Emili Sagol Creative Arts Therapies Research Center
at the University of Haifa, Israel.

Table of Contents

Part 1

Prologue..1
Dialogue..6
Termination..145

Part 2

Introduction.. 151
Chapter 1 – Childhood Sexual Abuse...153
Chapter 2 – The Uniqueness of Childhood Sexual Abuse.......157
Chapter 3 – Assessment and Treatment....................................169
Chapter 4 – Using Drawings with Therapy..............................174
References..181

Part 1

Prologue

Ziv

My name is Ziv. I am 36 years old. I am a social worker. My story begins when I was six years old, when my uncle, my mother's brother, started to sexually abuse me. The abuse continued for ten years, until I was 16 years old. At the age of 12, I began to care for my mother. I cared for her for five years until she died when I was 17 years old.

I wanted to write a book about my life experience. I looked for someone to help me with this book. I called Rachel and asked her if she was willing to help me write this book. We had a meeting and I brought all the material that I had written so far. After reading what I wrote, Rachel said that the material that I brought was incoherent. On March 2, she asked me if I drew. I said no. She asked me if I was willing to draw. I said yes. The drawing became the tool that brought out unconscious material, memories that were vague as well as repressed memories. Conflicting feelings toward the perpetrator such as love, anger, offense, ambivalence, and revenge were stirred. I found that I had a talent for drawing that I never knew existed.

I was in therapy for six years before meeting Rachel. I talked and wrote about the trauma, but I never really shared it or let myself feel it. I could not, as an adult, save that little girl. I could not be with the girl that was abused in that cage. I could talk about her, but I could not be her. Being her meant attacks of rage, eating disorders, inability to sleep, addiction to sadomasochism, difficulty concentrating, feelings of fragmentation, depression and detachment from the world. Sometimes, I could not even define who I was. For three months, I continued the drawing process, writing the narrative, day and night, and we had face-to-face meetings once every two weeks. From a chaotic and unclear point, except for the purpose of writing a book, I gained insights that enabled me to re-meet with my perpetrator 20 years later. Only this time, from a safe stance, as a grown up whose part of her history includes childhood sexual abuse.

The first part of the book was developed through drawings and narratives. When I drew the first time, I felt I was telling everything without words. Something in me could not stop drawing. It was the first time in my life that I felt I could see me. I was able to touch me without feeling pain and aggressiveness. Rachel asked me to continue to draw and a dialogue through the drawings and narratives developed. The drawings enabled me to talk about what the girl who I had been experienced, but they allowed me to see her, talk to her, to connect with her without rage and pain. I met with the little girl in a delicate, tender way. All my senses were activated and collaborated together and they became a new platform for insight. Emotion combined with cognition. Physical reaction combined with understanding. The abuse that once represented me, and was my whole identity, became part of my history; it was no longer me as a person.

At the same time, the change was gradual and sudden. Since I was six years old, my uncle used to sit me on his lap and make me watch pornographic films with him. All my life, I was addicted to pornography; I could not stop watching it. When I started drawing and the curtain of dissociation was raised, the abusive pictures were drawn and the pornography of the abuse was revealed on the canvas. I could not believe my eyes. I could not believe what my hand drew. Did I suffer this? I could feel and see what he really did to me, not to her, the little girl, to me. I managed for the first time to really connect to the child I was and to her pain, my pain. At the end of the therapeutic process, I stopped watching pornography and my addiction to sadomasochism disappeared. The process enabled me to meet with the perpetrator, to see him as he really is, and to free myself of him.

I was free. I released myself from the entrapment. My uncle was no longer my guard. He was not the strongest person in the world, not a lover, and not beloved anymore. And I am free. I was rehabilitated. Once I was a collection of figures, each acting independently. I had no control over them. Today I am Ziv, a professional, who has unique knowledge in the field of sexual abuse and trauma.

Rachel

At the end of October 2011, Ziv contacted me, introducing herself and asking to meet with me. She told me that she was sexually abused during childhood and she was a social work student. During our first meeting, she spoke a bit about the abuse and asked me to help her write a biography. It was obvious that there was more hidden material to what Ziv was able to present to me. I stated that my goal in writing books is beyond publishing personal stories. I have always been interested in studying incest and how treatment should be conducted; I wanted to add to the current literature base. Ziv agreed to be part of that goal. At our next meeting, Ziv brought a lot of written material. I tried to reorganize the material with her, which I found incoherent and unclear. I felt that we did not progress and feared that I would disappoint Ziv by telling her that the material could not be used for a book. Realizing that we needed to find another way to converse and knowing that for the last six years she had been talking and writing in therapy, I decided to substitute these forms of communication with drawing. On March 2, 2012, I asked Ziv if she was willing to draw. She immediately said yes. She drew two pictures and sent them via e-mail. She asked me to choose one for my office. This was the beginning of the therapeutic dialogue which mainly occurred via e-mails. Ziv sent a drawing. I sometimes sent it back upside-down. I asked her questions, and I asked her to add narratives. The relationship between us through the drawings and narratives became a daily activity; sometimes we corresponded day and night. I felt these emails were part of an intensive process and each one was in need of an immediate response. When Ziv did not get an answer for a drawing, she sent me an SMS, saying, "I sent you an important message, please read it." In the email itself, she added narratives to the drawings, and she asked if I had questions for her. She said that the questions helped her think. Sometimes she ignored some of the questions, yet the answer arrived within the drawings. Only later would she answer some of these questions in narratives or at our face-to-face meetings.

The process demanded total dedication on my part in terms of time to respond and understanding Ziv's emotional state. As we proceeded in the therapeutic journey, we both became more interested in process. We understood that this therapeutic process was different in terms of its intensiveness, the dialogue that included Ziv's drawings, my questions, her narratives and responses. I tried to avoid interpreting the drawings by suggesting to her to look at the drawings from different angles, or I asked questions regarding the symbols and their meanings. The symbolic content of the drawing usually preceded the cognitive insight. Three months passed in which the following changes occurred: symbolic drawings became more overt, and she was able to look at, feel, verbalize, and contain the abuse itself. Her perception of the perpetrator and her own identity changed; she differentiated herself from her perpetrator as well as integrated the various ego states of her identity.

The puzzle drawing was the first sign that we were heading towards the end of the therapeutic process. She had to choose at that stage between becoming addicted to the process and the intensive relationship with me and the readiness to change, meaning the possibility of meeting the perpetrator from a new standpoint. The decision was made: Ziv decided that she would not spend the next 30 years living under the shadow of abuse. When she was six the abuse began, and for 30 years she lived with the scars and the whole world was perceived through the lens of her abuse. She was in therapy for six years. The therapy was perceived as a contained, safe place, yet, in a sense, it was another entrapment. Now she was able to decide that the next 30 years would not be wasted being stuck in the past. The present and future would no longer continue to be a reflection of the past. The peak of the process was the meeting with the perpetrator. Although I have a lot of experience studying and treating survivors of sexual abuse, I never imagined how much this journey would teach me. I thanked Ziv for not giving up on me as a therapist, and encouraging me to pursue a way to successfully write this book.

Chapter 1 - Dialogue[1]

2.3.12

I would like to give you a drawing for your office. Which do you prefer?

3.3.2012

What Narrative comes to mind when the picture is placed at this angle?

---

1 Over three months there was a dialogue between myself and Ziv; mostly through e-mail. These exchanges included the transfer of drawings, narratives, and questions for clarification. From time to time we talked on the phone. Direct meetings were held every 2-3 weeks.

That is how I experience society. Even when I try to get out of the darkness, this is what awaits me outside

4.3.12²

3:30

3:32 Look at this picture upside down. What do you see?³

3:34 This is my dissociation. Everything seems calm and relaxed, but internally everything is falling apart.

---

2 Dissociation can be seen as a curtain that allows the concealment of relevant painful information from the abused himself and the world. The process of approaching the painful memories is gradual. For example, looking at the painting from different angles and allowing the abused to approach the threatening and painful memory, if there are the proper resources available at that specific time.

3 When the image is upside down, you can see that the figure becomes a symbol of a drop dripping from her vagina.

5:30
On one side, there is a desert. On the other side, there are ice floes. It does not matter which side I choose, I will die. So what is left for me is to walk on the bridge where his shadow chases me. I pray that if I continue, the view will change.

18.3.12

8:11
I will differentiate between being quiet and being totally silent. I think more than anything, I felt I was in total internal silence. It is a silence that echoes, which means that it is a deep silence that is very noisy. It is more than not talking, it also is not feeling.[4]

---

4   The face is the face of a man without a mouth; the lips are feminine, erotic. Neither of the two figures is able to speak. This once again represents the symbiosis and the lack of differentiation between the abuser and abused child.

14:30
We are at the sea. There is a nice view. Everything seems fine. This is a picture of my childhood. There is no separation between me and him. I am part of him.[5]

Look only at the top portion of the painting. What do you see?

Looking at the top portion of the painting, the blue is an angry animal, and threatening the yellow profile of a screaming girl.

16:00
A sense of freedom.[6] A sense that creation is a safe enough place to lower stress and arousal. This enables the child to express her pain.

The curtain is rising...

---

5 The image is actually composed of two paintings: the gray part, where two flat figures are visible in black and gray, and the top part where the symbiosis between the profile of the girl and an angry animal are expressed through the colors.

6 Physical death releases the bonds of dissociation. The dissociation is slowly dissipating.

19.3.2012

I told you I will draw the abuse. This is my private hell.

This is how I feel when I am not dissociating. This is how I have felt since my childhood.

I feel like I am being sucked into hell.

20.3.2012

7:30
I love this picture. The figure is imprisoned in the ground, but even though the lightning is striking through her heart, she manages to take the energy and fire it back.

This drawing symbolizes my anger, that there is no place to run, my sense of suffocation and helplessness.

God, who sees, not only does not help, but hurts.

The eyes are wide open, but they cannot see the one that they hurt.

22.3.2012

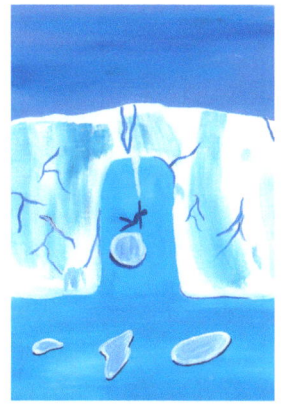

5:00
This is the most difficult drawing for me to look at. It really hurts my body!⁷

Look at this picture upside down. What do you see?
  Terrible Pain.

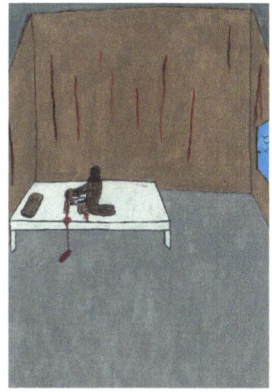

8:00
I know it is shocking ... But that is what I can't describe, because of shame and pain ... mostly shame ...

How can one give words to that??????? I do not know if I should continue drawing. On one hand, I want to draw what I cannot talk about ... On the other hand, it is shocking ... Who will want to look at this at all???????

---

7   Looking at the picture upside down, an erect penis is visible, and within it the figure is hanging. The figure is part of the abuse. The meaning from this is that the abuse is her identity.

When Time Stood Still

If they don't want to listen, then why would anyone be willing to see it?

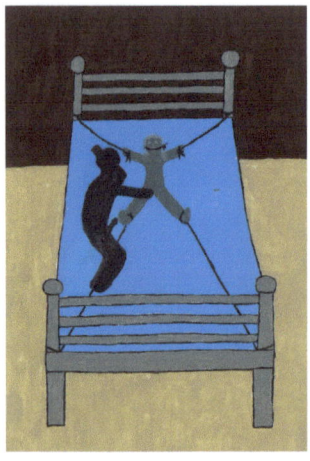

12:30
This is a drawing of one of the difficult moments that I had...

I was tied for hours. I remember every second...

What he did to me is engraved on my body. People can say that there is no hierarchy for pain...

Sorry, this drawing broke me to pieces...

24.3.2012

3:30
Funny, I try to make the drawings less blunt...

I understand that I don't really succeed in that. Well, at least the picture as it is in my mind does not appear on the page completely...

It is only in my mind.

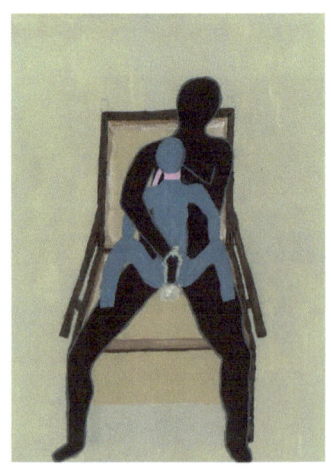

25.3.12

7:00
I know it might seem that this picture is less blunt, but for me it is very humiliating and difficult. You probably are asking, why the door … So, I would like to introduce to you the door to hell. Behind that door, no one sees and no one hears and no one wants to open it. What happened behind the closed door remains behind the closed door.[8]

13:30
This is a form of dissociation, but not exactly. Sometimes, when I had lost consciousness, I would feel like I was floating. I still remember this feeling. Funny, isn't it?[9]

The curtain of dissociation comes down...

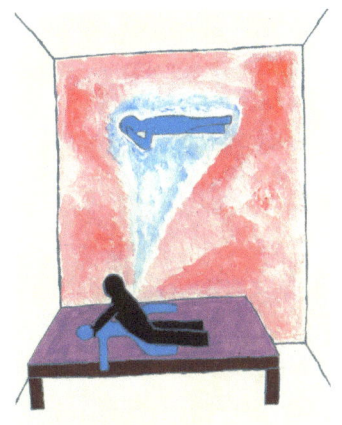

---

8 The door is closed, no one can hear, the shame and humiliation are overwhelming. The result: detachment. The curtain begins to fall.
9 Hovering above creates a separation between the body and soul, distance from physical pain, a protection for the soul. The professional term is depersonalization.

27.3.12

6:00
My therapist has been hospitalized for a week now. I need to be cautious and save my normality, because I am alone. She says, "Don't be frightened." But it is my soul, my mind, so I am cautious.[10]

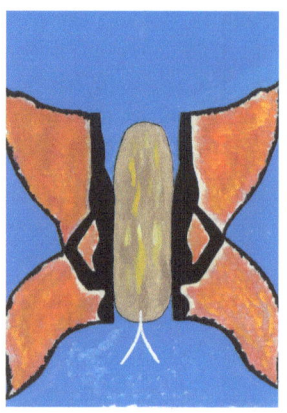

28.3.12

12:15
My therapist came back home from the hospital, so I started to draw again. It sucks that I feel that I am back at the beginning…

What frustrates me the most is that every stop makes me go back to the beginning. I am not able to start where I stopped…

---

10   When the picture is flipped, the figure is divided into two by the male sex organ. Splitting again and back to two parallel, differentiated lives.

Sometimes I feel that I have started the process many times because I could not finish it. On one hand, it is frustrating, but on the other hand, the process is so intricate that it is the benefit.

4.4.12

7:00

This was the mirror I had when I was a child ...

I always felt that no one wanted to be with me, even if I died ... At least, I had my flowers.

7:05
What happened at age 14?[11]
What happened at age 21?

7:07

At 21 I married a man who beat me. After 9 months, we were divorced.

11.40

Today, when we corresponded, I went back to the captivity and the meaning of belonging ... I felt the need to draw and it came out exactly how I feel ... The spider web is all around me. I like this drawing. And it saddens me to look at it. It is not really sadness; it is a deep agony.[12]

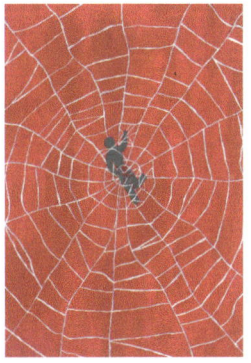

---

11   In the mirror, Ziv marks the 6 years of her childhood pre-abuse (Buried here, 1975-1981). The number of red spots around the mirror represents age 14. The number of flowers in the mirror also represents an age – 21.

12   The ignoring of the question about what occurred at age 14 indicates that the pain is not accessible at this point. The reference to age 14 in the painting indicates that the curtain of dissociation has been lifted.

5.4.12

4:30
I don't know what I painted ... I know this looks like nonsense ...

8:00
Look at the painting upside down and try to give it a narrative.[13]

8:20
I tried to draw what I still feel from the previous picture ... It is agony and mourning ... I know that the question that arises is "why do I feel agony?" ... I don't know ... I want to say that if I did, maybe it would stick, but I have no idea ... This morning, this feeling accompanies me ... I did not think that painting would make me cry like that ...

6.4.12

2:30
Maybe I had an abortion at age 14. Do you know something that I don't? I don't remember ... I don't. Maybe it is better to not remember ... It is enough that I know that for a time it was a very important role in the abuse; I was a prisoner of time ... and the hourglass symbolizes what is coming ... the feeling of anxiety of looking for a long time at the

---

13 The hands are the hands of the abuser. The figure within the drop is the victim. When the painting is turned upside down, the figure is drowning in blood.

clock and knowing that the time will arrive and he is never late.[14]
Please, can you help me?

9:20
It is hard for me because I connect with the emotion and my mind does not work. In this painting ... ummm ... I feel 1) I feel I was sacrificed; 2) something was taken from me, but I don't know what ... This is the struggle that I have every time that I need to enter once again into the darkness ... I am entering in complete blindness ... I am trying to get used to what previously occurred. But most of all, it's necessary to go back and forth into the darkness constantly ... it's exhausting.[15]

8.4.12[16]

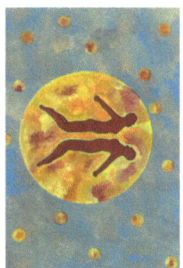

---

14 The hourglass represents the perception of time. Time does not help. It is circular. What has been will be.

15 A sense of emotional flooding, panic from the memories, resulting in exhaustion leads to the dissociation. The hands of the abuser, aggressively opening the vagina (the memory of how abortion was carried out came up in a later discussion).

16 The curtain comes down; the dissociation begins again. She returns to age 14, as seen in the orange spots surrounding the two characters. In contrast to the previous dissociative cycle (the figure, divided in two by a phallic symbol), this painting depicts the figures facing each other. Both of the figures are in red, matching the flooding memory of the red hands opening the vagina.

9.4.12

6:40
This is a picture of the book[17]. I can understand that whoever will look at it will see only a book, not something special. But this drawing is one of the significant ones ... Following our talk, I felt safe to draw it. So here it is.

1) I once wrote that he wrote in my book, because my book was not mine, it was his. So my book was full of his writings ... and this is what he wrote ...

2) I am coping with this - this is my book and although I can turn the page and start fresh, I feel tired and my pen is broken ... And even if I succeed to turn over the page and start again, my life history is already written in the book and there is no way to erase what was written.[18]

13:00
Whoever will look at this painting will surely say to himself these are the masks that I put on ... it's strange to think that I too thought the same until very recently ... So I thought about all of the theories ... And all that they had told me always led to the same result ... I have masks ... I'm not saying that I don't have masks! I am only saying that in this painting, these are not masks ... Suddenly,  when I drew this painting, I realized that every mask like this is my identity ... As opposed to placing a mask on my face ... My mask is my identity ... When I started to paint this painting, I

---

17 The words written in the book are translated clockwise: identity, shame, captivity, loss, guilt, pain.

18 Another cycle begins; the curtain rises and Ziv faces reality, where she, the victim, tries to see herself as separate from the abuser. She is examining the symbiosis on a sensory-emotional level and is trying to enter a process of differentiation.

felt an inexplicable connection ... During the process, I felt fear of understanding that these masks were much more than masks ... By the end, I felt the connection again and perhaps an acceptance that this is me ... Maybe the masks are different from one another, but the background (me) remains the same color with the same soul ... And the book – those are the words that were written in it and exist in every part of me, maybe not in the same intensity, but they are there and they are the connection between all of the identities ... Do you understand that in the book, everything that I do not have and everything that was taken away from me is listed ... Feelings, belonging, love ... And all that remains is to try to dismantle all of the difficult feelings into parts that will somehow be possible to deal with ... You know, people look at masks, but no one looks at the eyes ... Perhaps the masks are different, but the eyes are the same eyes ... No one ever tried to look at the eyes ... People always prefer the masks; even I thought that I too would prefer them ... Until I began to look myself in the eyes and I saw a whole world that had been hidden from me[19] ... I do not know if what I have written is understandable or not, but this is what I feel ... I need to share it with you and try ... after this painting, something calmed down; I feel relieved ... Or am I detached once again? I don't know ... but something definitely calmed down ... amazing.

10.4.12

7:00
Who is this? Who does it represent?

7:15
Do you know how hard it is to control this "mask"?[20] Most of my life I managed with it, most of my life I am trying to protect people from her ... It does not look scary, but I know what it contains ... I think that

---

19 The middle mask is red. Color-related associations are of similar emotional significance.
20 The red mask in the center symbolizes the centrality and power of the abuser as an introverted image in the inner group of the abused.

only my war against her makes me a better person ... I will explain – to control her, I need to be very skilled and I will exaggerate and say clever and witty things ... This mask, this is it and it is good and even better ... so it requires me to transcend it ... You talked about revenge, so for me, this is the ultimate revenge; not being what he created ... and with this statement, it is even more to not be like him ... In order to not be like him, I need to surpass him ... Eventually, when I look at the two of us, he indeed had the power ... But I have the strength ... When I think about how we are different, that is what distinguishes us ... Unfortunately, it is not something that I can say that I am proud of ... What should I say? That I protect human beings from what he could have been, but many are better because of it ... Who can understand this?

The curtain of dissociation is rising...

11.4.12

7:00
Good Morning ...

I first want to answer the question you asked me when we met ... You asked why did it end? I cannot say for sure – but I think that it was no longer a challenge for him ... I'm not sure about this, but he and I are so similar – this is the reason ... After he captured everything, my feelings and thoughts were removed from my body, it was already no longer a challenge for him ... the captivity ended!

In regard to the painting, what would you like me to expand? I ask so you can direct me ... I can tell you that the colors of the mask blend into the background because this mask encapsulates all of the masks that were in the previous painting. Those masks I took apart and created in order to cope with this mask ... I confuse the enemy. Ha ha ha, I needed to joke a bit – sorry. These masks were created so that I could redirect my ways myself, and to protect society from him ... I don't have to deal with the company ... I have no need for it; I was never part of it ... And I never received social recognition!!!!!!!!!!!!!! I'm not looking for social recognition by writing a book ... The painting of the mask mesmerized me, so I set it aside. For some reason, I cannot turn away from it ...

9:15
Expand, what do you mean by he "mesmerizes you"?

9:30
I think he is deep within me ... I don't fear him as long as all parts of me oppose him ... As long as he has the challenge to try to get to me, he continues ... I cooperated with this, but I did not say I was his ... The cooperation was mine and for me ... But when she had total submission, it was not cooperation ... This was of the heart, soul and mind, so there was no challenge, because I was already his ... The abuse was over ... It was all part of the game of domination ... The body is only a means to control all the other systems. As soon as he was able to take over ... The game was over ... I lost! It does not matter if the loss was inevitable ... the war that I gave was heroic but it resulted in captivity ... You know the phrase that goes "I do not take prisoners." It always amuses me that this is salvation for me, it is better to die from being captured ... When I get angry, I say "I take prisoners" ... (just to be clear, I have never done that) ... I do not know why I wrote this to you, but I am illustrating for you... And when you say to go capture him, then it is indeed to be addicted to him, but that is only because he does not leave ... or that I do not let him go ... I don't know ... He is embedded so deep inside me that I feel that his breath creates my path ...

13:50
I am sharing with you a painting that I am in the middle of ... Because something in it seemed important to me ... This has never happened to me before but this painting creeps me out for some reason ... I will tell you what I planned for the rest of the painting. I wanted to draw a raptor pouncing on its prey ... I just think it will erase a part of the painting as it is now ...[21]

---

21 You can see a blurry image, menacing, on the top portion of the painting. Upside down, the second figure appears.

13:55
Who do you see here? Creepy because...?

19:00
You're probably asking why I drew it so beautiful and powerful ... This is how a child would see it ... I think or feel that the previous painting was how I see it ... It reminds me of the painting of the flower being plucked ... I do not know why, but I had a similar feeling when I drew this ... I did the background and wanted it to be like a sunset ... and then I let the paint dry. I began to draw the falcon, but I couldn't. I saw his face reflected in my painting and  that downright scared me ... I felt that my fingers could not continue ... I shuddered. I felt paralyzed. This painting I sent to you right now ... it's connected to the previous painting. Only here, the girl is painting and she paints it differently, something else ... Me/She too draws something else ... I think she adores him ... And the painting of the flower very much reminds me of this painting because there, too, innocence is harvested ... love ... she loves him more than I do. And she is not able to think about him in a bad way ... Because that would mean that everything was a lie ... and everything that this girl has is his connection, his love ... If it is taken away from her, she will be left with nothing ... her past will be erased as if it never was ... The adult knows that there is nothing left that can be taken from her ... I know that I have the power to see him as he really is ... I know already that the past is not healthy ... but that means I'm hurting her, no?

21.10
The adult and the child are both parts of you, what system exists between them?

21.12
What a hard question!!!!!!!!!!!

My feelings towards her are changing periodically... I know that a portion of the abuse that I feel now is her abusing me... Her feelings towards him are very intense and she does not let me feel liberated from him... She echoes him all the time inside me... I often find myself very angry at her... I feel like she abuses me... I know she does not do it on purpose... but she hurts me ... and sometimes, I find it hard to contain her. I think she is trying to pass on to me the pain and the loss, the pain of being captured, the pain of being abused... I think that I make her mad when I cannot understand... although, I really try...

Now that she paints, this way gives her a place that I perhaps cannot give her. I facilitate, but it is not enough for her. The painting is a way for her to go back to her childhood and speak about what is happening to her... Writing this is completely delusional!!!!!!! I know... Anyone reading this will think I am... But, I feel the separation between her and me... I do not know when this separation was created, but there is me and there is her... mostly, I love her very much and I have a lot of compassion for her... And sometimes I do not... I think more than anything else, she is mad at me that I chose to be a victim and not to be like him... I understand her, but I do not regret the choice ... Today, I am no longer a victim, so therefore, my choice was right... She thinks otherwise... She adores him, so to be like him seems like the natural thing... Just like the mask that I painted... This really is delusional, I must note that I read what I wrote and this is delusional... but, I will leave it like this...

23.00

I completed the painting that I sent you... It is unfinished... this is the captivity... to be in a golden cage... The cage is beautiful, but everything else is akin to death... Or worse than hell... Without a doubt, this painting best symbolizes the captivity!!!!! You see what I see in this picture, right? The cage hangs around his neck, you see... The pathological symbiosis that I wrote about requires at least a period of abuse, a period of being a prisoner to some degree with me. I think to some extent that it was a mutual addiction… we talk about my addiction to him and that's ok… I just think he was equally addicted to me… Maybe not for me, but maybe he had feelings for… I don't know…[22]

24:00

I'm sorry that I am writing in parts… this is a continuation of my prior email… the connection between us was very deep; in order to reach such a level of connection it must be mutual… I can tell you that I learned from him… I learned addiction because of his addiction to me… I know others will not see it that way, but that's the truth… Think about how much investment is needed in order to imprison me in a golden cage… some feelings on one hand and spite on the other… the addiction is a learned behavior… I acquired it from him. I need to know if you understand what I wrote here??? Sometimes I write and only I understand it.

12.4.12

1:17
What is the relationship between Zahavit and Ziv?[23]

1:25
I am Ziv… I think my name angers her, this part of the captivity that was at the end of the abuse until age 22 or so… on the one hand, she was a very big part of my sacrifices… on the other hand, it was a very high level of control over impulses… This part silenced her and hides her completely from the present and from memory… And when I started to remember the abuse, it brought the child back to life… The thing is, she is so upset that she does not see who it hurts… I am not the victim that I was…

---

22 Who is the captor and who is the captive? The cage hangs on the neck of the introverted abuser?

23 In the question from the previous day about the relationship between the adult and the child, the distance was maintained by not labeling everything. Labeling shows that meaning is at hand. Later in the text, it can be seen that she approaches and moves away from a part of the ego that represents the girl: "I was a pretty girl, too bad that her childhood was wasted…"

I know that the girl is very unrestrained and that this part locked her inside and did not give her an opening to express herself ... only in the reconstruction that was ... I think that all of the parts that were captured since childhood want to return to him ... I think she is upset about this part because he captured her ... When I let her free, she just bursts out with all these emotions that just shock me ... There were so many feelings that I had never expressed and all of a sudden, out of nowhere, I was filled with them. I think that I am angry with her because this eruption came as a surprise. I was not prepared for such a massive explosion of emotions ... She takes the air away from me ... just sucks it in ... and I will return to Ziv. Ziv is the assembly of all the parts together, with very strong control over them ... she is the whole of all of the parts ... If each string of a violin is a part, then Ziv creates the melody ...

8:00
I think that the part of him that is within you was also addicted to you, and therefore, Ziv was addicted to Zahavit. Would there be Ziv if Zahavit had never been born?

8:05
You know, when I changed my name, everyone asked me all the time why and I said because it was too long and I wanted to shorten it ... But deep inside, I wanted to kill her; I wanted her to disappear ... I could not stand it ... her pain ... I thought that if I changed my name, it would eradicate her ... It got to the point where I could no longer hear that name ... it was like a curse for me ... He addicted me to her, not me ... She provides for all of his needs, I am the one who tries to prevent or attempt to prevent her ... I am not addicted such that I feel that I need to be the supervisor of their relationship all the time ... You see, they are so similar to one another that I feel most of the time that I am fighting against these two powerful beings ... and I constantly need to build myself up in front of them or against them ... It is mostly expressed in behavioral patterns and emotions ... it takes so much energy from me that often, I do not have energy for the world. I am busy all the time with my inner world ... as a result of the state of dissociation, I can move to an outer space. The dissociation can turn them off for a certain time ... I got used to

this circularity that sometimes it seemed unbreakable, permanently in motion ... I am constantly in motion, but others do not see this motion ... it is so frustrating and difficult. Outwardly, it seems like I'm not really moving. I am so tired of the race. So tired from the marathon ... the marathon that will never end. Every time that I reach the end, I discover that it is an illusion. And I start the race anew ...

8:20

I was a beautiful girl. It's a shame that all of childhood and adolescence were wasted ... too bad that the beauty was transparent ... through my eyes ... I know that I am fighting something that there is no possibility to win ... In recent years, I have had a better understanding of this ... I once wrote that all my life, I fight it. I understand that I am fighting with myself ... In this war, I have no chance to win, barely to survive ... I am angry  about their connection ... I am angry about their ability to love ... something that was taken from me ... something that is hard for me to create ... their relationship ...

13.4.12

10:30

It is enchanting, because it is beautiful to my eyes and anyone who looks at it will say what pastel colors, what calmness ... but be aware of the hand that rocks the cradle ... What I drew is not a part of the child or a part of him, this is mine ... And I think how easily everything was taken from me ... Like soap bubbles that just are touched and burst bubble after bubble consistently ... how easy it is to reverse the life of air ... and when I say easy, I mean without feelings ... not necessarily in practice, because this actually takes effort ... but without guilt, without shame ... as if each bubble that was burst[24] was a part of me, my childhood, innocence, feelings, and in their place, he infused the most difficult emotions ... In the end, he left me with nothing ... Sorry, not nothing, he left me with a lot of difficult feelings, patterns that are almost impossible ... an unrealized lifetime ... You know I could be anything, but I'm not. I'm starting now until I get where I want ... I always saw myself having a lot of influence and success ... I know I am clever, smart ... and it feels wasted ... It sucks ... And it's not just beginning now, it is starting from a very big minus and trying to make up for the minus ... But OK, this is the situation and I am doing what I can ... I did not give up, which is also good, right? And I'm sorry for my reaction to when we were talking about my good traits; it really doesn't do me any good ... In Ziv, there is all of the innocence in the world ... I have never hurt someone intentionally ... I never acted upon my maliciousness in order to cause harm ... I could not live with the guilt if I did it ... because of this, I am very vulnerable, which goes against what everyone thinks – that I am a steel wall that can't be knocked down ... It's not true; I am a very sensitive, very caring, very warm person ... This is exactly why I am careful with people ... Anyone who gives me his heart and soul, I wrap this gift with cotton so that nothing bad will happen to it, even accidentally ... They think that I do it to please others, once this was true; today, I'm doing it for another reason ... the feeling is different ... I do it wholeheartedly ... and I protected everyone from childhood and you know what, I'm not sorry; it has made me a better person. Maybe I was victimized; I say was because I am not now ... But OK, it is better to be a validated victim ... I prefer feelings of guilt, pain, shame about the aggression, abuse, and soullessness ... How did Frankl say it? "Anyone who has been wronged does not have the right to do wrong back" ... The only difference is that in the (concentration) camp, they had each other to remind them of the simple truth ... I only had myself ... This changed me into a person with a different strength ... At least that's how I feel ... I know - what a lovely picture ... Some-

---

24 The red hand: the red hands that are depicted in each painting are the hands of the abuser.

times it takes me a while, sorry ... but the soft colors of its beauty ... that talks about innocence; everything was there ... this is my source ... and it is wonderful in my eyes ... And then he came into the picture and he exploded the parts of captivity ... He hurt and blackened them ... But somehow this picture has hope; a lot of hope ... If I successfully, slowly but surely, scrape away his black layers, I have a chance to restore some of these soft colors ... Maybe they will not be the same exact colors, I'm not really sure, but they will not be black ... I think I can do this and I succeeded, though sometimes it appears that truly everything is only black ... But my core was not black ... not a drop of evil ... how do you say it ... "Clean and Pure." So the race did not yield anything and also the treetops did not, but it's now pruning season, no? :) It's hard work, but possible ... Anyway, I feel that for me it is possible ... And probably, after what I just wrote, I will return to the beginning, but what does it matter .... There needs to be small islands of hope in between ... no?

10:45
How do you feel about the process?

10:46
Good! Suddenly I can see emotions that I did not even know were there ... It's rare to see them, no?? Usually, I feel emotions, they are abstract, but to see them, this is an amazing experience! I feel the ups and downs emotionally and mentally ... Yesterday I noticed that I was flooded with emotions. Today is a bit relaxed ... The situations from the street manage to overwhelm me quickly ... But now I am relaxed. Especially sharing with you, this is easy for me ... not the sharing itself ... but that I shared with you ... I share with you the most intimate and private parts of myself ... and I have a desire to share more with you ... It's not a simple process to detect things, not just to deal with them, though deep down, I know them. I have many moments of fragility, it is often difficult ... A sense that the soul splits in order to deal with the process ... There are paintings that I want to bury myself in and some paintings that give me some peace ... This really occupies all the colors ... And that's just what I see and I see flat paintings, unlike you ... I only see what my conscious paints ... The painting with the cage was the first time I saw the sub-

conscious ... it broke me because it gave me a sense of helplessness ... and dread ... I felt that my subconscious slapped me and told me "You may not see me, but I'm here!" like the girl telling me "I'm here" ... Today, I see it as I've never seen it before ... The last painting made me feel closer to her and love her ... Suddenly, I saw her as she really was, not what he created ...

13:00

I really don't know what I drew here ... I didn't think, I simply moved the brush ... But I will tell you what I felt when I painted, a vortex that pulls inwards and outwards ... Sort of like what happened to me when this process started, I started therapy more than 6 years ago ... I pulled in strongly, but pushed out not as strongly ... And every entrance or exit breaks me completely, and then there is a spiral that assembles me anew again and again ... But really, I do not know what I drew ... I'm sorry that's what came out ... [25]

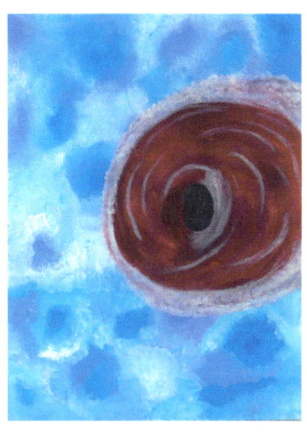

14.4.2012

5:30

I remember this picture ... here already he was abusing me. This was a trip he took me on ... He took a picture of me ... I look at this picture and I don't know how to react to it ... You see how small I am? How can you abuse something that small? I asked questions that were never answered ... Just look at how she, sorry, I, look at him? This is a glimpse of love ... All of the pictures that he took of me they are with the same perspective ... In all photos taken of me, I do not smile. Always there is only sadness and pain in the eyes,

---

25 Circularity of pain, separation, anger, detachment, entry and exit from dissociation requires a lot of energy; it prevents progress.

except for the ones that he photographed... What does that say? I remember that day he walked with me, and played with me, and we had a picnic together. I remember I had fun with him... I'm beginning to think that maybe I suffer from Electra complex ... That day he did not touch me, just love ... I loved these days ... Despite the constant fear that something could change, I still loved them ... You see, my mother never left the house; she was stuck at home all the time. Only for errands did she leave [the house] ... But to travel, almost never ... once in a blue moon ... That was her life ... And he, he traveled with me, taught me things. He was very smart. I remember my conversations with him were adult conversations ... not conversations of a child with an adult ... He taught me to be an adult, to act like an adult ... He taught me from a very young age to be a woman ... And my mother's role to teach me how to be a girl, it never happened ... After she became ill, she expected me to be an adult ... I think that it was because of him that I was able to cope in a mature and effective manner with the treatment when she became ill ... He was my role model, not her. And he taught me efficiency... Does what I wrote make sense?

5:45
From the last set of paintings, I remembered that I had fantasies of killing him. I thought about burning him alive and looking him in the eyes while he burned. Me, not him. I have not killed anyone. Suddenly, I realize that parts [of me] really want to harm him, basically, leaving me with him. My conscious wants to hurt him, my subconscious wants to keep him with me. You see, I always felt I was living in hell. I clearly knew that I was a bad person who did bad things and that God did not want it. The fantasy to burn him was divided into two reasons. First, I wanted to see him burn in hell, like me. Second, if I take him with me to hell, he will then be on my territory, where I have control. One the one hand, I wanted to take revenge on him and where better to take revenge than in your own home? And hell is my private home. On the other hand, this is to get him back and to keep him with me. I suddenly realized that all the good or bad actions are the result of loss and longing ... All of my paintings were of loss and longing, except for the one painting with the hands, the first one with the storm ... I still feel that this is a

different loss ... It is important to me that you know that there is a part of me that believes in love and not his love ... I learned to love through my therapist and to be loved. Sometimes, the types of love blend and create emotional chaos. I can say that today I am able to love and to be a partner, I share out of love. It is emotional and for someone who has not had feelings like this, like me, it is a beginning.

15.4.2012

12:00
The pain in my childhood led to dissociation ... This I know. The intensity of the pain from my childhood, from the harm, from the abuse, is in direct correlation with the strength of the dissociation. The more the pain strengthened, the dissociation deepened and lasted longer. Within the dissociation, the pain continues to exist even if on the outside I do not really express it. When the dissociation fades, the pain again takes its place. For the time allotted, I can exist with the pain. When the pain reaches a certain intensity, one which I can no longer tolerate, the dissociation takes over again ... and so on and so forth ... a vicious circle. There is no possibility to stop it ... I want to share with you ... and so that I'll remember to tell you ... I'm addicted to pain. This I already know ... I thought a lot about why ... and it seems that this one reason out of many ... but an addiction to pain serves at least two important things:

1) I have no surprises – you know, when I was little, the pain came as a surprise and I cannot let that happen again. I hate surprises – good and bad. This for me is not being in control ... so that the pain that continues all the time lessens as another pain arrives.

2) The dissociation depends on the pain. I am dependent on the dissociation, and the pain is actually a powerful sequence of the dissociation itself. Perhaps, the addiction to pain occurs due to the need for dissociation.

16.4.2012

8:00
I continue to paint, but it is really slow ... I felt the way that I

am painting is a pattern that I really don't like. There is intensity, and then I begin to overflow and break ... You see, I talk all the time about mental and emotional dissociation, sometimes even intellectual dissociation ... But there is also a cycle of physical dissociation ... Even the body dissociates ... Even the body reaches a moment where it cannot tolerate the physical pain.

8:05
Let your fingers go at their own pace, do not push your body, you are allowed to slow the pace and gather strength.

17.4.2012

12:30
This is a painting that I was stuck on for several days ... This is what came out, despite the fact that I need to see him in person, face to face ... There are drops of blood on the black paint that you cannot see at first glance ... I do not know what this painting represents, well, maybe I know ... but ... I cannot connect with the emotions right now; it is hard for me to associate with it ... I am starting to leave the

dissociation ... yesterday I was so furious that it woke me ... And no, there was no reason for such a level of anger ... Nor did I take it outside, but I felt inside that everything was suddenly turbulent and came alive ... Now I am calmed down, so I guess I'll slowly make the emotional connection ...

12:45
Who has the key?

17:50
This is a type of process that I can play.[26] I play until they begin

---

26 You are playing for whom? Who hears? Who does not hear? What is the tune?

to break. The strings are torn ... therefore, they need to be fixed. This is the cycle ... I think that I tried to reflect through the painting the sensation that I perform and then I create the cutting ... it is not simple; I need to connect them all and then continue from the place that the cutting was created ... Did I explain this well? This is the dissociation. The strings are the feelings and they are not connected and therefore I need all the time to connect the strings over and over again.

17:55
You are playing for whom? Who hears? Who does not hear? What is the tune?

18.4.12

4:00
You know, it bothers me that I don't draw anything about my mother ... I do not feel anything towards her??????? It's not clear to me. It's not even close to there ... I remember when she was very ill, at the end of her life, and she asked me to pull the plug, she did not want to suffer any more ... Part of me thinks, why me? Is that what she thought of me, that I'm a murderer? Am I so evil? Today I know that it is not so. But then, this was significant ... you see, it was between being a murderer and disappointing the person that I wanted to please most ... any decision, its implication would disappoint her ... I chose to disappoint her ... Today, I think, what type of mother would request from her child, who is still young, to pull the plug? I wish I was mad at her, I wish ... She was never a mother to me. I learned everything by myself. This has its advantages. I became what I chose ... I am trying to find this place in my childhood where I am able to say that there was someone else other than him ... That

I will not feel that he was the only one there. Unfortunately, there is no one... you know how frustrating it is that the person who ruined my life is the only one that exists in my memory... I don't remember my mother... What child doesn't remember his mother? I do not remember anything, except for her being sick ... There was one time, around when I was 14 or 15, she had to go to chemotherapy and it was decided that I would go with her ... She was scared to go alone. And I had vaginal health problems and could not get out of bed. I remember the pain I felt, like knives cutting into my stomach ... I remember she was angry with me that I was unable to go with her ... She told me that she was relying on me to go with her, and she would not go without me. None of my brothers volunteered to go ... I remember going with her and sitting there for three hours with writhing pain inside. On the outside, no one could tell anything. And I remember that I felt in any moment that they would hospitalize me for labor... But I absorbed the pain inside... Sorry, I know this is not related, but I wanted to share ... this keeps me up at night and stays with me all day ...

19.4.12

12:10

A picture is worth a thousand words ... There are three ways to look at this painting. One, it is his hand that moves me ... Two, the hand symbolizes my situation in childhood; the hand is all I had in childhood and adolescence and this is how I felt inside and out ... Although, inside I had more freedom of movement, but outside, the situation consumed me, requiring me to follow the structured rules ... There was a sense that the situation had trapped  me inside it... He is a part of the situation; he is the one that created it ... The third option is that this hand is me and therefore, I dominate the part of the child ... Though, in reality, I give her more freedom of movement than this picture suggests.

20.4.12

7:00
I think of all the times that they tormented, abused, seized, and murdered me ... From childhood, I have the ability to rise from the ashes and to revive myself over and over again ... This painting reflects this ability ... This life taught me so many bad things ... I was able to take all of the bad things and make some of them livable and some of them beautiful ... I drew the picture to show you Who is Ziv ... I have a lot of parts. Some are hard, some are less so ... but this is my strength, to revive myself every time anew. Maybe they killed me, but they never succeeded to kill my essence ... He was good, but I'm better than him![27]

When you turn the painting, what do you see?

---

27   The strong clawed bird is hurled into the air by a strong and mighty wind that comes from within. This is the same spirit you could see in a number of the previous drawings (The lightning hitting the small figure, the captor with the cage around his neck). The image of the abuser is also internalized in the victim's identity.

When Time Stood Still

8:00
What do you see when you look at the two paintings?

13:10
These two paintings, to me, are very similar and not only are they similar, they also convey the same concept, just from a different perspective. The first painting that I created was of the hell that I found in him. This is how the child sees the abuse. She feels trapped in her hell ... The second painting, this I painted. I captured her ... This painting is more cognitive ... It's strange to look at the two pictures and see that two different parts painted them ... And what a difference there is between the parts compared to their similarities. In both of them, the child is imprisoned ... to see that I did to the child, what he did to me ... sudden insight ... to see what I had done to her. To understand that in all of my pieces, he exists, only in different variations ... Astounding! Today I was in therapy and spoke to my therapist and asked her if she would agree to meet with you ... she said that she would be happy to ... so, if you want ... and you asked why I want this, then I don't want it, I think that it's necessary and this is important ... and I gave her permission to talk to you about everything.

13:20
When you look at these two paintings, what do you see?

13:25
I think that this is the continuation of the painting that I just sent you ... In childhood, he imprisoned me in a golden cage ... but this is more than imprisoning a person in a cage ... He went with me everywhere and I with him. And the cage wasn't closed, so through it, I saw the world through his eyes ... slowly, his world turned into my world ... Deep inside, without anyone seeing ... I was an integral part of him ... And to see the world through his eyes, or even replaced what I saw ... Everything changed to be in his colors ... until finally, I changed to be the same color. I didn't just see them; they became a significant part of me. And the painting of the phoenix reflects how much the transformation was his success.

21.4.12

14:50[28]
The ground is bleeding. Her blood is dripping through the eyes ... Something is raging and burning deep inside my stomach ... I know I should write more. My head is totally blacked out ... sorry.

14:55
And again the indication of age 14

---

28 There are 14 stars in the painting, which hints to an incident that occurred at age 14.

When Time Stood Still

16:37
I know it's not the most beautiful painting ... But it was really difficult for me to draw it and I was determined to finish it ... When I was with him, the whole world did not exist, except for him ...

17:05
Look at these three paintings, what do you feel?

17:10
I think that the three paintings show the process of socialization ... the process of absorption ... I actually do not know if I am sure ... I suddenly realized ... The spiral is more than repeating in the paintings, it returns in other parts ... The return of the spiral tells the process of the socialization! The parts are not divided by age, rather, the status of the captivity ... Do you understand what I am trying to say? Wow, this is big ...

18:50
My emotions have calmed down a bit so I can write the narrative for the paintings ... 1) in the drawing where I am hug-

ging him, there are feelings of lust and longing. 2) This is just a hunch. I feel like I'm the one that doesn't let him go from the embrace. Such a grip is hard to remove... Moreover, this painting strongly connects me to the painting with the spider web... If in the drawing of the spider web he is the one that is clutching me, now I am the one that is clutching him... you see, he imprisoned me and therefore, there were no feelings of longing and loss... But now, something inside of me feels like he is missing... Not at the level that I would go and do anything about it. Just to be clear... But this painting very much connects me to him... I remember this picture and although it looks erotic, it symbolizes for me the embrace, the touch, the heat...

20:10
Do you remember the first time we met I told you that the loss was the most difficult? If they had taken me out of the house, would I have been able to survive? I've thought about this a lot. The paintings and the reflections on them connected things together for me. The reason why I don't think I would have survived it is because it would have been during the formation of my self-identity. If they had pulled me out during the process of my identity formation, it would have disjointed me. I would not have been able to survive... all the time people ask me how I survived. I think that I survived because I stayed in the same place and, perhaps this will sound strange, but the continuity was traumatic, in terms of stability, routinely traumatic... the formation of my identity. Traumatic as it may be, an identity all the same. I think because of that, I managed to survive. He would take me out of the house before the process was complete; I was homeless within myself, a bag lady in my body... I think about this and how shocking it might seem, but I came out of the abuse with his identity. An identity of the assailant who helped me survive and function. Today, I can say that it has taken me time to break everything down and start to build anew. Today, I have the power and the ability... If this were not so, we would not be able to have this conversation at all.

22.4.12

I repressed this stage, so I will return to it now, if you allow

me ... In my previous painting, I embrace him; that is the stage before the last one. This painting, this is the last stage ... us together ... the connection between us... what no one wanted to see ... or to believe ... This painting is from my adolescence when I no longer cooperated, I was already there ... You see, in my mind, to cooperate with this would be just to ease the pain. This does not mean surrender ... but there is that moment of surrender. It's impossible not to surrender ... and this is what happens when surrendering ... And you should know, the background was painted first. I tried four colors for the figures before I connected to the wine-color ... I do not know what it signifies, but it seems important ... this color has something appealing ...

23.4.12

5:30
Turn the picture upside down and write a narrative.

5:45
The picture that you asked me to flip ... I see a funnel ... I think that that is the abuse. It is the type of funnel that is designed to get exactly what appears in this painting ... And the contents of this funnel consist of me and him.

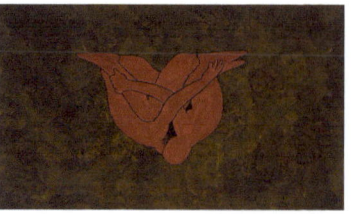

10:15
This is my bubble today ... today, no one will be able to pop it ... because it is full of thorns ... but I'm inside it. I'm protected ... I know that it has its disadvantages. But it has one advantage and it is more important to me than anything. This bubble protects

me ... you see, the previous bubbles were from my victimization. This is another bubble ...

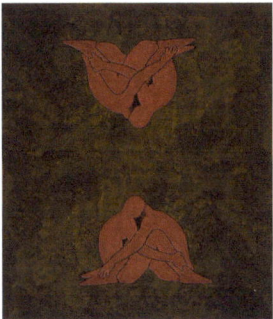

10:20
Again we return to age 14, see the number of thorns on the outside?

Look at these two paintings. What do you feel?

What is the significance of the time?[29]

10:25
I was connecting the painting of the hourglass to the painting of the figures ... there is something that drains to some peak ... and somehow, the hourglass connects me perfectly to the same feeling ... You have the painting of the hourglass, right? Or do you need me to send it to you ... Have a wonderful morning.

24.4.12

4:30
I think that this is the advantage that I have when I say traumatic stability and that the process is completed ... I have the ability to leave equilibrium on the path to change or to return to the previous equilibrium ... I have more confidence and control over the process. If they had taken me away during the abuse, they would have taken the balance away from me ... because I had nowhere to return to in order to start anew.

---

29 When she was with him, time stood still. It was just the two of them at the peak of intimacy (distorted and painful). The meaning of time in the drawing is that nothing else existed but the relationship between the child and the abuser.

4:35
Are you interested in meeting with him? Do you think it will help you with your process of change?

5:10
I really do not feel that meeting with him will change me ... I do not need it ... I know that I will not receive an apology, so why do it? And you know what? I don't want his apology ... I do not feel that this is a part of my path or my process ... In another five years, I think I will be free of the parts that bind me ... I want to be a lecturer! And I will be. But most of all, I would like that the past not be the core of my being ... And I am working hard to create a different core focus ... Rachel, for me, the book is my purpose ... Palahniuk said "Everyone dies; the goal isn't to live forever. The goal is to create something that will." And the written word remains forever ... for me, the book is my meeting with him. And the answers to all of the questions I find during this process is the way I know him best. There is no need for him to be here physically. He exists inside me ... I prefer to remember him as he was.

6:15
I know that I write from outside of myself ... So I will go into myself for a moment ... you see my mother ... this is a picture of my brother's wedding ... She was made up with a beautiful wig ... and look at how she looks ... this was during the relatively better time of her disease ... take off the makeup and the wig ... (by the way, I set the wig, it's nice, right?) ... and think about how she looked ... She deteriorated a lot over time ... and I do not remember her as beautiful or even as a mother ... I remember disease and her without decency ... He and she were the most important figures for me ... I must remember at least one person with decency ... and it is doomed to be him ... What I also asked you to forget was that the abuse was sexual; I prefer to remember him as he was. I do not think that I emotionally can accept the difference ... For me, to see him now without the dissociation ... that is to see a tremendous difference that I do not have the ability to handle ... I simply don't want to ... I'm happy with the situation as it is ...

7:30
I do not know what I am feeling, but I am able to write about loss

... because when someone dies, then he dies. It is impossible to see him, there is only longing that he will return ... This is a part of the loss. I have clear knowledge that this is just longing ... This loss is something else. To see him with feelings of loss, that's a bit cruel, even for me ... for me, this is beyond abandonment. This loss, unlike ordinary loss, is not final ... this is loss that sticks ... just like dissociation. Between life and death! I truly love the girl as a girl. If she gets older, even the few children that I have in me will disappear with her ... There is a song by Iggy Waxman that comes to me when I think about him ... "I have nothing to say to you beloved murder, I love you, I miss you, leave me alone." In regards to the differences, I make changes in my rhythm and in places where I feel safe enough ... It's not easy to make changes, because every part that I change, it changes all of the pieces of the puzzle ... the picture changes. Everything is different. So obviously, any kind of attempt to make a change before I am ready causes me anxiety ... not anger, anxiety. But this is why I do not want to meet with him; it's not connected to change. I really do not want to meet him ... it's not right for me ...

7:45
Who is talking to me?

7:50
I wonder the same thing ... I wanted to ask you, do you recognize what part of me writes to you, because it's a little difficult for me to identify ... I think that all of the pieces together are being very careful in this place ... I only know for sure that such a meeting will certainly not occur ... Who from the parts of captivity is directing this, I have no idea ... I also rely on the intuition that tells me not to do it ... and I am very at peace with this decision ... I know that many recommend mediation; I do not think it's for me ... Actually, I know it's not for me ...

12:00
I still don't have a narrative for this painting ... I know that I love it and that it is very special in my eyes ... and it took me hours to paint it, but it was worth it. I wanted to ask you for a small favor, if you could please stop talking to me about meeting him, that would be nice ... it does not do me any good ... talk to me about

everything, ask me whatever you want … but I do not want to talk about the meeting … maybe it's suitable for others, but it is not suitable for me … I really want you to feel free to continue to ask me questions …

12:20

These eyes are the same eyes? Whose eyes are they?

13:40

At first glance, when you look from above, you see angry eyes … But if you look at them a little differently, at a flat angle, the eyes are much more relaxed … I think that the anger is a more internal part of me. I actually feel relatively fine … that's the problem, you see, I don't identify these feelings so quickly … I feel great, and then later, like a thief, quickly and quietly, comes an emotion that is very difficult to control … and it's surprising, because, in spite of that, I am aware of its existence, it does not come without warning … but I'm really pleased that this time that I painted the anger, it was not alone, I was there, too … I don't think that this time it's a sign … I think this time I surprised him! It sounds like combat tactics, I know ... which is exactly what it is! I also feel that this background is me and this time, I mastered it ... I did not let him go loose, not within me or outside of me ... I gave him a place to roam, but it was controlled ... this surely sounds bizarre to you, all the thoughts that I write ... I sense a flow in my writing now ... this is huge progress for me ... Usually, there is a tendency for these feelings to control me ... this time it's different ... I will bring the painting to the session so you can see the faces; it's pretty amazing ...

25.4.12

5:00
Look at all of the pictures, what do you see? What is the connection between them?

6:30
The first painting is attributed to the beginning of the process of captivity and abuse ... the second painting, of the volcano, is already during the abuse. The phoenix is the final stage of captivity. The painting of the tigress is the balance between my essence and his identity ... the first painting – there are massive intrusions and there is no way to escape the penetration of rage, but this is his rage ... the second painting – the volcano is the part that is full of the anger that he infused into me, which created an emotional flood inside of me that just seeped out ... but I always worried that the leakage would be measured, all of the anger still remaining inside of me ... I wrapped my rage in a huge rock. The third picture – of the phoenix; I think that this is the peak of my inner rage ... But there also is hope in it because I think that precisely, in this part of the process, there is a lot of hope because I have learned to use the rage positively ... I think that this is related to dissociation. I learned to channel it through the anger ... there is a process of death (dissociation) and then comes the rage that brings me back to life ... And then there is the final painting – the tigress – which is basically my ability to control the rage. Not only to use the rage, but to actually control it ... Even if I cannot detect its arrival, I still have an internal system that already successfully deals with elements of surprise ... And the transformation of the penetrating rage (this was his identity) - my absorption of it - finding an effective use for it - and being released from his rage (and from his identity) and introducing my identity.

15:15
Isn't this a beautiful dissociation????
I really enjoyed painting the autumn leaves ... I'm still not writing a narrative, because I still do not know why I associate with the painting ... I can only say that it brings me peace ... and finally, these strong colors (red, orange, yellow) infuse me with peace ... a part of total permeation ...

26.4.12

5:30

Look at the symbols of these three paintings. What comes to mind? What do you see?[30]

5:50

The painting of the autumn leaves really connects me to the painting of the hourglass ... There is flow, movement. Looking at all the paintings, it seems to me that this is the process, the interaction of the rage with the dissociation ... something that is built until it breaks down ... but it can be reversed, which in my opinion is very important ... it is not just that the rage leads to dissociation ... The dissociation can lead to rage ... this is a cycle ...

6:15

I remember that I was becoming emotionally overwhelmed and I dealt with it pretty well ... but then something was said that instantly threw me into a wall and I felt rage ... this is exactly like that conversation in a group that said that battered women are stupid, stupidity and some other words that are not worth mentioning ... and I remember sitting in the room and I felt the rage flooding me ... until the moment that I thought that if I responded, it would not end well ... I remember that I just sank, sort of like the autumn leaves ... or the hourglass with the rage

---

30 It is important to understand the meaning of time for the abused: Is what it was what it will be? Does time heal? Does time worsen the situation? Is there room to grow in terms of time? Is there a future? A present? Is the past the present and the future?

buried underneath the sand ... I felt that it was better to detach ... I listened to what was said, but I didn't really listen ... I was present, but not really present. I remember that the teacher wanted me to talk and I preferred not to ... they always wanted me to talk ... but they didn't understand that I wasn't always able to talk ... I did not respond, I left the room ... the rage did not disappear; the dissociation just locked it up ... it is very fragile in a situation like this ... this rage in a second did not come to me in a second; it is something that builds up, until I cannot contain it ... I have a very specified time until it builds ... but then the reverse process begins ... I dissociate until it reaches its peak, and then the rage drives me away from the dissociation. After these situations, I disappeared for a few days inside myself ... and then I started to feel anger that fills me ... I started to see this situation in my eyes ... and feel every blow and the humiliation ... I'm not talking about that situation, not really ... I left the detachment ... and the power comes back into balance ... until the next time.

It is very difficult for me to connect to the situation ... because it happens all the time ... from childhood, this is the progression, this is not something that happens once ... this occurs all the time. It is like a cycle that never ends ... For example, in childhood, it waited for him to arrive ... the anger built out of helplessness ... When he was with me, it was the disintegration of the rage through the body ... and then the dissociation was during the act ... then it returned to outrage over what had just happened ... this is a closed cycle ... it never ends ... and then you take him out of the cycle ... because the world and society are abusive so this is just switching it to an external cycle ... maybe you can direct me a little? Rachel, I want you to ask me general questions. It helps me.

7:20
Do you feel that the anger towards him you have put on yourself? Do your feelings of anger towards him cancel out your feelings of adoration towards him? Are you mad at me?

7:25
I'll tell you why I'm mad ... because I tell the truth and I share the biggest secret ... and I admit that I inherited his identity ... which is directly related to the place of my monster ... I think that

the girl is just angry that we see him all the time as a monster ... I think that again, we do not know what she feels ... So what if I acquired his identity? He wasn't just a monster and for me, he wasn't a monster at all ... Yes, there was evil. And yes, a part of him was a monster, but not all of him ... this is not just that we see him as a monster, it's that it turns me into the same thing ... and I'm not an abuser! So what if I look like him? That doesn't mean I'm like him ... And somehow, I feel that when I tell the truth all the time, they attack me ... but not you ... so I do not have anger towards you, you understand ... you know, all my childhood I had to conceal, to hide, to lie, to manipulate. And to be exploited ... and therefore, I've been trying to break free and get the truth out ... they tell me indirectly to shut up ... and again, I feel like they do not see me and they do not see the girl ... the girl loves him and I will not take that away from her ... No one expects to be thought of as an angel, truly they don't, because he was not ...

But when the girl experiences the reactions against him, this hurts her ... they do not harm only her, but how she relates to him ... therefore, the rage accumulates and it is inside until it explodes out or relaxes. Your questions do not anger me and they do not change my way of thinking ... If you look at the first email that I sent you this morning, it alone connects the hourglass to the painting of the autumn leaves ... you do not intervene with the process. I think that you have part of it ... this is OK ... in the end, I will write what is inside my gut ... Rachel, if this is not my truth, it won't be written ... I promise you :) and I am truly sorry that you felt that I was angry at you ... it's funny, you might be the only one I'm not angry at right now ... you know what, I will not quiet it and I will not shut up ... whoever is unable to accept it, they shouldn't be there ... I am angry at Miri, my therapist, because in the last meeting, I shared with her what I feel ... and what I think about identity ... it wasn't easy for me to share this ... you know, all of this confessing makes me balanced ... To admit that his identity lies within me, and then that it even managed to help me survive ... this is not an easy confession ... and I showed her the paintings of what I see ... and she was just not ready to accept them! And then I found myself trying to explain to her what I feel and think for the entire session ... I felt that there was a war in the room ... it wasn't that I fought it, this is what she fought ... it infused me with rage ... I was angry at her, but I asked if she was angry at me ... I realized that I project on her what I feel ... at the end of the meeting, she still tried to convince me that what I think is not true ... but in the end, she accepted my words ... she said that it takes her time to process ... but I left the meeting really hurt ... I felt that she didn't understand me ... it is difficult for her to accept that I have him in me ... I realized that she sees him as a monster ... that's natural, I'm not able to change this ... she doesn't know him like I do ... When I condemn him, I condemn myself as well. When they are attacking him, they're basically telling me that I am not good enough ... if my identity was created through him, then I'm also a monster ... when they have this attitude towards him, they take away from me all of the good things too ... the good things that enabled me to survive him ... to alleviate the feelings of the girl ... The girl cannot tolerate this attitude against him, because he is all that she had ... and including anyone who knows that I experienced abuse, automatically sees him as a monster. They will even say things like "I wanted to kill him, to hurt him" ... curses and labels ... and the girl feels like they are talking about her as much as him ... So this is the anger that builds up ... that paralyzes ...

9:50
I feel like there is something wrong with me. I don't feel like other people feel. All the time I feel attacked. They say that this is victimization, but that's not true. I am not a victim, certainly not today. I feel attacked. All the time I am under attack. They try to fix me ... You can only fix broken objects. So I'm an object and I'm broken? All the time they tell me that he abused me ... I know. I do not need anyone to tell me this. I live with this 24 hours a day. But whoever says this to me equally abuses me ... This statement says: you poor thing, and you're a victim and you're broken, so let's fix you. I am many things, but I am not broken and I am not a victim. Every time that this happens, all of my parts become paralyzed with anger. Sometimes I am paralyzed from hurt. How many times can I hear that I am not good enough? Whenever I try to create something new, they always judge me. This is exactly like when I consulted with my seminar teacher because we had to do a group project. I told her that I was going to speak about sexual abuse and my experience.

Because this was important and I wanted to speak about it. Her response was, "Ziv, is this the business card that you want?" And how am I supposed to respond to that? If I get angry, they will say, "Ah, she is angry, because she experienced incest." Or they will say, "She doesn't know how to respond." In actuality, what she said to me was, "Shut up." They try to break me into pieces: there is Ziv, and there is Ziv that was abused, they are not the same person. Today, she is someone else. I am not someone else. I am Ziv who underwent abuse; this is a part of me. The main feeling is that there is him and there is the family. Society is like the family - silencing, exclusionary, and abusive. So I return to the safe place with him. It's not because it's safe for me there, but because it is familiar to me. There I know how to manage my emotions much better. There I have already experienced the abuse, so I am familiar with it and I do not need to experience over and over again new abuses.

When I think about age 14, I am filled with great loss. I have no idea what it is. I create a new part in myself following this loss. This part is stronger physically and mentally, the part that helps me to survive this loss, a very blatant part of his essence. I think that's when I needed that part. The part that keeps me from crashing. My dissociation in regard to what had happened is much more massive. For example, when my mother died, I felt the presence of this part. It just completely neutralized the pain and created action.

10:30
Who are all the people?

11:05
All the people around me are abusive and unhelpful. A few are not. I know that they all think that they are trying to do good, I do not think that it is out of malice. You know that the road to hell is paved with good intentions. Only they send me to hell, and do not go themselves. Believe me, it is hard for me to think about it in good terms. It is not easy for me to say there were good things about him or that I felt love for him. That I depended on him. That, at some point, I really needed him. That he was all that remained from my childhood and that was all that was within it. They do not understand that I do not remember any-

thing else or anyone else other than him. I also have difficulty with this. I know that if I take him out of me, I have no past! So I need to create something from this abusive past that is positive. The truth is, he also was good to me, not just bad. You know how hard it is to live with the feeling that the person that murdered you is also the person that made you the best! It's very easy to judge from the outside, but I have to live with it, not anyone else. I have all of these parts inside me that feel and think differently from the other. Particularly with respect to him. I need to balance all of the emotions and thoughts. I have to connect all of the parts that are sometimes contradictory and disconnected from each other and sometimes it seems like there is no way to bridge them. And I manage. Even the girl has more than one part. There is the part that hurts and is angry and abused and there is the part that is connected and loves ... and all the parts want me to see them. I will address them. And myself. I know that it is a miracle that I did not go completely crazy. The distance between the fall to madness and survival is small. And I survived. I think to myself that I am a much stronger person. I have internal strength. So, how am I still connected to him at this level? I have a lot of anger inside of me that's so big because there are all these parts that want me to shut up and do not want to reveal secrets because of what the disclosure will cost me. I, myself, do the action, but every time, a different part of me is paying the price. This is a war in itself. And until I create balance within myself and try to tell the truth, there will be some external factor that will silence me, that will say words that will immediately make me angry.

27.4.12

10:15
Parts or figures?

10:40
That is the point, I do not have figures; I have parts. I have never felt that this is not me. My dissociation never has completely detached me from myself. I do not have multiple identities. Time does not disappear for me. Time is transient in detachment, but nothing happens in it. These are the different parts in the captiv-

ity and socialization process. Look, for example, on one side, the girl wants people to see her and to see what she went through. On the other hand, she feels that they are invading her intimate space. It is very difficult to explain that I consist of different parts and that I am a different variation of them. It is difficult to live with this. Do you understand? Take, for example, pain. The girl's pain and my pain are very similar, but they are not the same. Its rage is not the same rage. The girl's rage is impulsive; for me, the rage is measured and controlled. This is what it is like to be made up of separate parts. I think that the majority of people are made up of consecutive parts that work with each other. For me, it's slightly different. I need to identify which part feels what all the time. I must adapt myself, so today's Ziv has the same feelings. This is much more than managing emotions. But to manage them, I first need to begin to identify them. There are parts of me that do not want me to talk because there still is shame and guilt. There are parts that feel that there is an invasion of intimate space, and then there is anger directed at me. There are parts that are supportive. Ultimately, I am the one that controls all of the parts; therefore, I do what is best for me. This does not mean that I do not have internal struggles. Wow, I do not know if what I have written here makes any sense. Truly, I tried. It is really difficult to explain something that seems impossible to explain in words.

11:10
I feel like you are talking from outside yourself. I wonder, is this my sensation or is it a sensation that you are passing on to me?

11:20
I will try to draw for you what I wrote. Perhaps through the painting it will become clearer… This painting has sat inside me for a long time, but I was not in a place to draw it… the girl is angry at me. This is what I feel. You know what? Even the part of me that was created during my adolescence protects me. I think that the part that protects me feels a little helpless because it is not in a position to protect… You know, as soon as I reveal the secrets, it becomes more difficult to preserve them. I am the one that writes to you, not the other parts, and I am trying to explain and perhaps because of this, it is hard for me. Currently, I am

not connected to the rest of my parts. I am detached, I know. I am writing from outside myself. But for me, the outside is no less important that the inside. When I am outside myself, I am not totally outside. All the time I am a little inside myself. What I really try to convey is that my parts are fragmented. Each part stands alone. Each part and its behavior. And each part belongs to a particular dimension. However, there is no change in my identity. I am always me. There are changes in my behavior and my emotions. There can be a situation where each part will respond differently. It is not only difficult to understand but difficult to explain. I just want to make it clear that I do not have a completely different identity. Probably some of the different parts are becoming more dominant.

14:30
I was not so invested in the details of the painting because the message was more important…

14:35
Can you flip the picture and write a narrative?

15:10
The painting of the figures – I flipped it and the first thing that I felt was I was missing a figure … I do not know which figure, but she is missing from me and she was bright green … I feel that I have in me a lot of parts and they converge into a single gray image, because gray is not seen, not really. It is from such a neutral color that it is not present, yet it contains

all of the colors. All of the figures are very tied to him; he is the vertex because they were all created because of him. My feeling is that all of these figures were brought into existence in order to deal with him. He is abstract and has no body, but his presence is like a tornado that creates my inner spirals. These figures are his by-products and I am found exactly in the middle – between the figures and him. And it is him that, from the beginning, creates the effect of the shadow. Without him, these figures would not exist. The hourglass, for me, was a sense of being buried and the attempt to stay alive and survive, even though all the time it felt like time was over. It really reminds me of my childhood. The sense of the entrapment of time. Every meeting I had with him would end and then my anxiety would begin to wake. I knew that time was running out until the next time. The feeling was that there was no time to heal from meeting to meeting. This aroused my difficult physical reaction. I did not have enough air in me to physically heal myself. The anxiety was intensified as time went by. For me, the captivity of time was very significant. Everything becomes extremely limited. Time is the main importance of a day. This hourglass has the desire to break it. To end this captivity of time. Even today it is entrapped, maybe a bit differently, but similar. If I am in dissociation, or moments not found in the abuse, there is an automatic internal anxiety, because I know it will come, something will happen, trigger, the floating feeling that something will happen, and then it will return. Sometimes I confess that I simply stayed abused, because I've already been there and there time is not ticking. And this is the internal ticking that you find in the mind ... I am missing one figure.

16:10
Where was your father in this story?

16:15
He was not there.

Abba (Father),
    I do not know where to start and I do not know how to write this letter without hurting you. You are a good man. I know you never meant to hurt me. I also know that you love me and that

you fought to bring me into the world. Now, I realize what I didn't understand when I was younger, maybe because I didn't have the strength to see you, or maybe because I was unable to see you. It is clear to me now that you were not in a good situation with Ima (mother). I know that you loved her and you defend her fiercely, even today. You no longer have to defend her for me. I know she controlled you, and she never let you grow. I could not deal with her. No one could deal with her. If she was alive today, I would be dealing with her. All of my childhood, you were not there. You were at work all the time. My memories do not include you. You were supposed to be a person of value and meaning for me but someone else took that role away from you and you did not notice. I am angry at you. I have no reason to forgive you. I know that you didn't have any idea. As far as you're concerned, these things do not happen. So why do you see that it happened to your daughter? I'm angry at you. You abandoned me at the moment I needed you most. I lost everything and was left with nothing and all I have left is you. But you chose to move on to a new life, with a new family, and forgot that you had a little girl. I was so hurt and I was left alone to lick the blood flowing in all directions. And then, when I reminded you that I was there, after you left me home alone for days, you did not come to comfort me but, instead, to take me from my house to a new place without even asking me. I feel like you are not my father. You ask all the time if I love you and I answer yes, because I don't want to hurt you, but I don't love you. I respect you as a father. Do you have any idea of what I lost in the past three years, and I survived, not because of you, but because of me. I lost the only person that saw me, I lost my mother, I lost my family, my identity, my house, and what was left of me, which was not much. And you, you were not there. I remember how much you were not there. You were my last hope. After you, I stopped expecting. After you, I understood that I was alone in the world. I wanted to die, I really wanted to die, but I didn't want to hurt you after the death of Ima. She took my death away from me and I hate her for it. I was mentally and emotionally broken and you didn't see it. You kicked me out, I was seventeen and a half, you threw me into the street because I embarrassed you in your new family. I will never forgive you for what I went through on the street, never. The nights that I slept starving, in the cold, in stairwells, on the beach, in the rain, in fear of dodgy men. It's a wonder that I'm alive. I will not forgive you. You were able to stop it and you didn't; neither you nor my brothers. I do not belong. You threw me into the street and it is impossible to return home from the street, home was no more. I didn't have a home anymore. My house burned down. You pushed me to get married, because I was living with someone out of wedlock, and it was so shameful for you. You pushed me to marry an abusive man, you want me to forgive you for this? Even when I had decided for myself to try to get a divorce, I asked you to come with me to the Rabbinate so that I wouldn't be alone; you refused. This "No" still echoes in my ears. I am not your little girl anymore. Your little girl died a long time ago. Now, there is a different model that is broken, disassembled. If I didn't look like you in the mirror, all connection between us would be accidental. In all of the moments of terror and fear, I never thought of you as my savior and I never cried out for my father. When I started to write this letter, I didn't know who I should write it to, you or him, because he was more my father than you were. I am much more similar to him than I am to you. He was stronger than you, smarter than you, more sensitive than you, and more loving than you. The other thing that differs between the two of you is that you did not hurt me directly and he did and I thank you for that. You never exploited my body. I know that you have a soul, it just didn't find me. You are a good person to everybody, except to me. Do you remember when I asked you to help me finish school and you told me that you didn't have any money to help me? I only asked for 2,000 NIS to complete my degree. I was so hurt by your answer. Later, I discovered that you helped a foreign family and financed their child's Bar Mitzvah from your money … instead of helping me. And you want me to tell you that I love you? The mental health officer explained to you that I went through abuse. Do you remember that you asked me if that was it, and when I didn't answer you said to me to shut up so I would not destroy the family? So father, I have no family, my family died in the street and also my family from the street died, I am alone outside and alone inside. Your God took everything away from me. I am an old person in my soul and in my emotions. I am older than you. I will not forgive you for this; you took everything away from me. I am not going to stay quiet anymore. I do not belong to you. I wrote the book to make sense of everything. Why did you ask about him?

6:30
Because you wrote that you were missing a figure among the figures and you thought about him when you were asked to be interviewed on TV, you were afraid he might get hurt.

28.4.12

12:05
I have no idea what to write about him … I am still overwhelmed with the letter.
Thank you, Rachel.

1:30
Unlike the rest of the family, I have compassion. I am not vengeful, and I will not do anything to hurt him. Moreover, none of my brothers speak to him, just me. I do not have the heart to take this away from them. Before the book is published, I will meet with him. He does not need to be surprised. I have no desire to hurt him. You know, I thought that I had already moved past my anger with him. Now, I understand that a part of me did not let go of that anger. But I have the right to be angry. I will always be someone who cares. That makes me a better person. It reminds me of what is important. Today I am doing this from a much more complete and mature place.

2:30
Look, my mother was not a bad person, really. But with my father wrapped around her finger, life was not easy at all. He will

never admit that, but she was bossy and quite the seducer. I do not want to be like her. I do not want his experiences with me to be like his experiences with her. I am not like her. I do not use my power to hurt others just because I can. My strength is precisely the ability to not harm. He is still my father and yes, I feel compassion for him. There is a part of me that is not angry with him and wants him to have a different experience in his final years. I do not want his love now. It is already too late. I do not believe in it. I am not able to forgive.

2:35
What is it for you to "forgive"?

2:40
I think it is dependent on the price that the injury cost me. You know, when I do something, I'm well aware of the price and therefore, it is my choice to pay the price or not. It depends on when I need to pay the price for the actions of others ... If this is a mistake, I am able to absorb it, I forgive. But, if this is something that left me scarred, I cannot forget. There is no chance that I will forgive a trauma. It also depends on my relationship with that person ... I will forgive a friend much faster because I have no expectation of it from him. From family, that is something different. I've given them so many opportunities. Every time they hit me and used me. In my eyes, to forgive, it is not to feel the burden of when I think about him as a person or when I see him, it is to feel calm. Not to feel angry and try to hide it, but rather not to feel angry at all. When I speak about anger, I'm not talking about regular anger, I'm talking about rage. To forgive, it means not feeling suspicious all the time with that person, not having the expectation of harm. In my understanding, to forgive is to start anew. A blank page, clean. And the problem is that with the people that are significant to me, it is impossible to start a new, clean page. It is a book that is filthy and torn.

29.4.12

7:00
Are you able to write Zahavit a letter? To address her?

7:30
A letter to the girl[31]

You know, years ago, I tried to suppress your existence, not because I hated you, but because it simply hurt to remember you. But you were there. All the time. I even tried to be blind. As I thought of you, I realized how I could not really suppress you. A part of you was present and existent every step of the way. I think to some degree that you have more strength to cope, much more so than I did. I abandoned you in order to survive. I apologize. I disappointed you. You have a lot to say. Comments through me. You do not have to scream anymore. I know that they will not listen to you. I remember that they did not listen. I listen, so speak, express. Only, don't scream. Because when you scream, I disappear. This is how you taught me. Try to be less angry at me. I really try to be there for you, and it's difficult. Your pain is suffocating me. It's paralyzing. I remember all of the feelings you had during childhood. I'm not able to forget. I wish I could eliminate the pain, but that takes time. I'm not giving up and not being discouraged, for you. You do not believe in love. I want you to know that I love you very much. I think that you are a smart, clever, sensitive, very special, beautiful girl. Yes, even if you don't see it, you were a very pretty girl. And today I am very proud of you. You survived for me. I owe you my life. When I begin to remember you, I see you with me in the room, but I cannot tell anyone because they would think I'm crazy. Today, I don't see you, and it's a shame. On difficult nights, at the beginning of the therapy, I was alone all night and sometimes you were alone with me and, at times, the pain was as one, I felt your pain so clearly and I didn't understand how you coped with it. I adore you. I know that you're not going to abuse me or hurt me. I know you're just trying to convey to me how you felt and what you experienced. I apologize if I can't always contain you. You see, since childhood, more things have happened, and they want a place, and this is not like you are less important, because you are very important, only that they always want to talk and express themselves. And when I walk away from you, it is not forever, in the end, I will return to

---

31 Ziv still does not call the girl inside her by her name; instead, she distances herself and calls her "Girl." Ziv still maintains "she and I."

you because you are the root of everything. And I let you do what you want when you are inside of me, even if you think that sometimes I prevent you, I am not preventing you, I'm just relaxing. But you know that on the outside, you need to behave differently. Today, I am not alone and I cannot allow you to treat others the way you treat me. I am a part of you and you are a part of me. You already are not a secret. I do not hide you anymore. I need you to trust me that I will not hurt you. I need you to stop trying to hurt me, so I will not hurt you. Forgive me for abandoning you for so many years. Now, I am here to stay. You only need to choose me.

30.4.12

5:00

I know that you want me to write a letter to my mother and to him, but you'd be amazed, they are less significant to me, even more than I thought ... it's really weird. I hope that it's okay that in a certain sense I write to myself.

The letter ...

I know you best, the most complicated part. I remember that you have a lot of good and I know for a fact that you never gave up your essence. You have not hurt anyone and you did not do anything bad to anyone or to yourself. I think that you need to thank the girl because she taught you to survive and, even more than that, she showed you the inner good that stayed with you. And yet, you are the part that is without feelings because when you were on the street, it was impossible to have feelings, all emotion can lead to death. I know that most people see this as just a saying, but those who were on the street know that this is not just a saying, it's the truth. And I remember that everything that passed through your hand, you did not give to anyone, and nothing got too close to you. You kind of have an animal instinct for survival. And this instinct is emotionless and it makes it very difficult for me to deal with you, because I have a lot of emotion, not just a little bit. And I didn't understand where you had the courage to do what you did, things that today I wouldn't dare to do. And suddenly I realized that you did it because you do not feel fear, because when you don't have feelings, you don't have the full range of emotions. And this was not courage; this was a

When Time Stood Still

lack of fear. Today, I was in Tel Aviv; I do not like to travel to Tel Aviv. And I passed a familiar place and I thought about what you did there and how you entered that place without fear, without blinking and without your friends, only because it was necessary. In truth, I think that you've done courageous things and no matter what the cause was that enabled you to do this. But today, it is very difficult for me to deal with you, because I am unable to tolerate your robotic-ness, and this can be looked at as post-trauma, but you simply disconnected emotions completely in order to survive, this was not because of trauma, this was the basic instinct to survive. Today, I struggle with you about indifference. Good god, nothing bothers you, you can be in a situation where others are dying from pain and you, you do not even move from your place because you do not feel pain. It's scary; it scares me. People think that I'm strong and nothing scares me, this is not true. I am scared of a lot of things, but your indifference scares me the most. And the craziest thing is that you do not feel anything and you have no emotions, but today, I feel every emotion that you repressed. And you have no idea how much you repressed and what you repressed. I know that you don't feel anything, but I feel for you, and this causes me to crash again, every time. Everything that you have been through, I go back to your place. Only then you experienced it without being there, and now I am experiencing it while being fully present. I have to say, it is lucky that you did not feel because you would not have been able to survive. And yet, sometimes, I am scared by your indifference. Today, I am functioning as a complete being, and when you appear, you knock me off the balance that I so gently created for myself. You can disable me for days. It's difficult because I realize that I am unable to move from this. I can be found in all of the parts that are in me, I am always present, but with you, it is most difficult. You see, I prefer full pain, full pain in order to feel anything. I am simply addicted to pain. You know, to see all of your experiences is to see them clear-eyed, and when I see them in my way, I totally collapse. You are the only one that divides me between pain and difficulty. Your survival instinct leaves me with everything. Without me, you wouldn't exist. I would like for you to take some time for yourself because you were there and you need to cope with it. You do not allow me to talk about what was there; you've captured me without giving me a way to leave that place.[32]

6:30
You know what just occurred to me, that the number six has a lot of impact on my life. When I remember things, it's amazing. Did you know that all of my relationships lasted exactly six years? Only now with my girlfriend I broke the cycle. But I always said that six years is enough and now I need to finish. In six years, the relationship is exhausted ... Also with work, it is always six years. Even in the current relationship, I had a crisis six of the years. I remember it very well ... And I was in therapy so I could get through the crisis. What a situation, I do not understand how I could not make the connection until now! What a missed opportunity!

I want to share with you, there is a part (identity) that is a little difficult for me. Yesterday, when we talked on the phone and you said that I did not just arrive to you now. You know that I chose you, right? And when you asked why, then all of the parts chose you, and that is my intuition, when all of the parts agree. So then I know that it is the right choice.

10:00
This is my emotional spectrum. I think this characterizes it best.

10:30
Look at all of these paintings, what do you feel? Think? See?

---

32 The girl that was held hostage by the abuser became the representation of the abuser within herself. In order to cope with this, she created an additional ego represented by Ziv.

You see the metronome, it is the same shape as the bridge. This is related. My emotional spectrum corresponds to my relationship with him. It is impossible to know if he is chasing after me or if I am chasing after him. If we look at the bridge upside down, then I am running to him. On the other side of the metronome is changing emotions, outbursts of anger, and also detachment, which comes because of the attacks of rage. There is movement, but really it is limited, because it is from the same base. I have the control and power of the emotions. You know how to limit the context that I find myself in. They are like the bridge, flanked by clear boundaries.

1.5.12

10:20
During my teenage years, I came by this song. Today I decided to return to it after years of not listening to it … I think it reflects everything … I like the version with David D'Or because of this. There is a change from first person to third person … I marked for you what was meaningful for me in this song.

Although, a whole lot of it is meaningful for me.

I see in your eyes
That nothing is important
Just you, me and you, again and again
I see in your eyes
More than anything –
You would close me in,
If you were able

Would you build me walls
Would you install my lights
So that I will have light

She sees in your eyes,
It is written in big letters, you would
Let her, forgive everything

She sees in your eyes,
She sees everything, as you would
You love her like no one else can

I was wandering around between the walls

I would make in them shapes –
That I would have the sky, I see you
In your eyes
I see everything
You would wrap me in a house and warmth
I see in your eyes
I see everything – only
You do not see me amidst the blue

I walked hours ago

And it was good for me outside the walls, good
Me outside the walls, longing for
Home

2.5.12

4:30
You asked me to paint what I felt after listening to the song ... I'm part of the sky so I do not see myself in the blue. If he did not wrap around me then you would not see me at all. It is slightly like seeing me via him. Or better yet, not to see me without him? You can ask questions if you want ...

When Time Stood Still

5:10
And age 14 comes up again[33]
  And the world does not see you without him?

6:00
I would not see me without him[34]. I wrote but just do not remember where ... I'll find it if you want. That I was made transparent and that changed everyone into being like me, transparent ... Because a child learns from how you look at him ... And if I was transparent, I could not see me ... And he was the screen between me and all the rest of the world, then something in his color actualizes me to myself. Truthfully, in the painting I ignored the others, it did not concern me as I painted. I think that when I was with him he wrapped me in his color which is what separated me from the rest of the world. But it made me separate.

14:30
Hi Rachel,

I enjoyed my time with you today. It was really fun to talk to you. I sent you a short clip, I recorded myself on the way home, that way I would not forget anything. Transcribed for you ... I would really appreciate if you sent me your reaction to it, if you do not mind.

Rachel, I transcribed word for word what I said, there was no break between sections, they followed one after another. It was important for to me to write them in sequence because I think it helps me understand how my brain works. This is how I integrate between things. I can start with one topic and move on to another one entirely. And somehow it all comes together in my head. Let's start from the process. In terms of the process I can say that the process started with talking and through talking there exists the possibility to run away. It's okay to run away because sometimes you need to escape. But it's much deeper than that. In the writing and the storytelling, I am writing about me and talking about me, but I do not see me. I think that the experience of trauma causes the lack of visibility, and, in some way,

---

33 The number of stripes in the girl's hair is 14.
34 Zahavit did not have visibility without him. The one who hurt her was also the only one perceived as loving and caring.

speaking and writing about me is simply not enough, I wanted to see me. I think the paintings are me. I manage to see myself in them, not parts of me, but me in my entirety. And they form one cohesive whole which is a lot easier for me to deal with because I see it, I feel it, and this is what I have to say about the process. Now, I'll switch to the song. The song "I See in Your Eyes" connects me to exactly what I said a moment ago. There's a sentence in which she sings "I just do not see me in the blue" that's the point that no matter how hard I tried I simply could not see me. And that's what I felt when I was a child. Amidst this situation, I could not see me. Another part in the song "I left hours ago and I like it outside the walls" and the question is, what walls? Two meanings: it is good for me outside the walls - this is the break between our meetings, when we weren't together. But it's also basically when he was with me, I sang to him that I left hours ago. He is with me but I'm not here, I'm not with him. That was my interpretation of this song. Today, it symbolizes something a little different. The dissociation remained the same, which is astonishing. Even today, I'm stuck in the abuse and the escape to dissociation is my respite. But when I am dissociating, I miss home, and, in a sense, abuse is my home. But there's also another meaning, there's also hope, at least for me. I do not want to return to the abuse. In my thoughts and in my soul, there is captivity, yes, but it's also a song that symbolizes change now. If I bring myself back to situations of captivity, it is because it is familiar and safe. So the song symbolizes for me the change that I no longer want to return to external captivity. And I'll say that the return to captivity from a known place of safety and security is not exactly true, it's part but it is not essential. There is, and it sounds strange to people, but I'm sure whoever has experienced captivity in life like I did knows what I am talking about. In captivity, there is something that is not found outside of it, and that is freedom. There is a difference between freedom and liberty, inner freedom is something that is experienced only in captivity in the most bizarre way. Captivity makes you withdraw into yourself, and you find your inner freedom, one that is not found outside yourself. Most people think freedom is the ability to do what you want when you want, this is not freedom; it is liberty. Internal freedom is something inexplicable; it only exists in a feeling. And the desire to return to captivity is to search for this freedom again, because, after experiencing it, it is very difficult to give it up, it becomes significant in many ways. And I can say that today I have freedom even outside the circles of external captivity, with others. I managed to create some sort of circle of captivity within me which gives me the ability to connect to this freedom, so I do not need to hurt myself with others. And I think it's another one of the reasons that I was not hurt much, relatively. I am not involved in too many abusive relationships, even though I was once was, I do not deny it, but that was before I found this inner freedom, which I so dearly missed. And today, after I found it, I do not need it anymore. And this seems to be something important that needed to be said.

3.5.12

6:40
Being see-through is not a good experience for a child. This transparency becomes part of his identity. When I was transparent, well, everyone around me was also transparent. They did not see me. It is circular. I seem transparent, so they do not see me, and so on. The only way I could see others was the same way that he saw me. My transparency experience was split: on the one hand, I was not seen, and, on the other hand, everything was seen. I always lived with the feeling that I should be hiding myself. That they shouldn't see everything. Everything is to see him inside me. To conceal me was to hide him. If I hide him, then the abuse did not happen. It cleansed me in a certain way. Me of him. When you are clear all colors fade out of you. But that means all colors. The good, the bad, feelings and thoughts, the identity of being, everything becomes transparent. And transparent is empty, but not just empty, it's empty existence. When he was with me, I felt seen. Not seen in an ideal sense but rather visibility. For me as a child that's what it was, and I took what I could get. A deal with the devil. As a girl, the loneliness just enveloped me all day, every day, it was suffocating. It was like putting my body in a vacuum and sucking all the air out. I waited to be with him, not for the sexual contact, but for him, his attitude, his touch, yes, even his touch. It already didn't matter that it hurt; the main thing was to feel some kind of contact. You become addicted to the touch, because it's the only contact. So, there exists an addiction to the

attention and the feeling that there is someone out there who just notices your existence. It would be better to fill the transparency even with black, just so that it would be filled. And he filled it, and with him the loneliness decreased. It is clear to me that even with him I was lonely. Now, I understand that he did not see me, rather, only the body. But as a child I took what I could get. Even if it was something negligible.

6:45
Like the painting of a small figure inside the blue?

6:47
Correct. :) It is to be swallowed up inside of him.

6:50
When I think about the whole process I went through, I understand that there were transitions in the process. Crossroads, some of which I created myself and some I arrived at with the help of my therapist. But the amazing thing was that my process is based on senses. I'll explain. Suddenly, it came to me, so I'm writing to you because things have a tendency to disappear for me… It all started with speech, which uses the organ used for the sense of taste. It continued in writing which is the sense of touch. And sight. It moved on to painting, which requires using all of the senses together. It is to talk, to see, to touch; it activates the sixth sense, which to me is the subconscious. But what's amazing is not necessarily the transitions themselves but the fact that using one sense leads to the use of a different sense, without canceling out the previous sense, rather it is added to it. It is as if the soul connects through the senses… it protects itself from painful feelings, so it adapts gradually to the senses and emotions… I really do not know if I explained myself correctly, I hope so. The process is very special for me. I think in trauma all the senses need to

be expressed together. The connection between the senses is the connection between feelings and thoughts. It provides the ability to integrate both the trauma and the inner parts.

13:40
I do not yet have a narrative... but it is so beautiful!!!

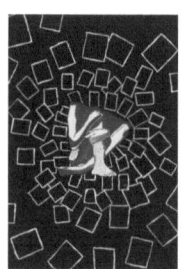

14:00
I am trying to write, but nothing will come. I am choked up with tears. I think I need more time.

19:00
I am undergoing a very complicated process through my paintings. All my life, I was not able to grieve for anything. In therapy, I began to grieve, but I was missing a tombstone and the paintings are a kind of tombstone. It sounds horrible, but it is a form of release to know that my losses have, and I have a place to go to and mourn them... the tombstone spent a lifetime inside me and finally I am able to copy it out of me... Clearly, that the paintings are not only a mourning process but, but they also are... do you understand?

4.5.12

3:30
Sorry for the time... That's how I feel every time you ask me about age 14. I'm trying to scrape off the wall and I can only scratch it, it just will not peel. I have said, "I feel that this is an abortion." I just do not remember for sure.

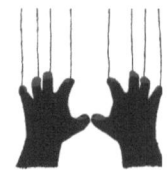

4:00
Try to paint what you wish had not happened.

7:00
I don't know what to write about this painting... You asked me to paint what is better off left unknown... this is what came out.[35]

7:15
Turn over the last two paintings and write a narrative.[36]

 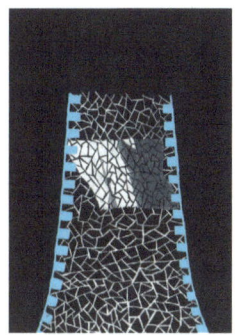

8:05
The last two paintings look like a bowl that has been turned on her mouth. The painting of the arms, it looks like grief and mourning are spilling out of the fingers. And in the drawing with the zipper, it feels like something died inside, broke inside and it cracks from the inside out. In both the paintings, there seems to be a divide as if I only have permission to enter so far. It is astonishing that I created barriers for myself. It is always thought

---

35 She was asked to paint what she wished had not happened, and she painted what she would rather not know.
36 Looking at the painting of two hands scratching the wall upside-down, the hands are holding a penis. The second painting represents the vaginal canal with a shadow of a tiny figure appearing in it.

that my walls are for the people out there, which is not true. My walls are internal and radiate outward toward the environment. I feel that she will not let me in, not really. Who is she? She is who I was at 14. She built a barrier and the key is with her, and she will not let me near. She does let me feel what she was feeling, I experience this grief. But she will not let me see. Unlike the girl who just wants me to see her and what she went through. The fourteen-year-old does not want me to see. Not her and not what she has experienced. I think she was trying to protect me … But the feeling remains the same feeling with no face, it's like reading a book without words. I know there are words, I just do not see them. And now, I sit to paint that grief, and painting takes time, a lot of time, just like you feel with grief, time passes slowly … But there are things that I remember. I remember that there was no birth control ever … I remember that he was not careful … And the feeling is that something died inside of me, but what I do not know …

14:05
This is the grief. This is the way it feels, and that's how it looks … What amazes me is how beautiful such a harsh emotion like grief can look… I feel that flowers fall off of me and I do not have the power to prevent this molting … Although I try very hard, I cannot really … I love this painting because it reflects exactly in every detail how I feel the grief … Isn't it beautiful?[37]

14:15
She is alone in her grief. There is no one to hug her, but herself, and she is already 15.

---

[37] The red color represented the hands of the abuser in previous paintings. The hair symbolizes the same drop dripping from the vagina. After her abortion at age 14, she remains a whole figure, turning her back on the world, alone, bleeding and hugging herself.

5.5.12

5:30

I want to write you something that has been in my thoughts. It's not that I do not believe in love, I have thought about it in depth. I do believe in my way ... You know, sometimes, people tell me I'm like a robot. It is not true; it is even a bit offensive on some level. I am a person with a lot of emotions. Even during difficult periods in my life, when I was supposedly devoid of emotions, they were there. I know that they were there because I experience them today just as they were then ... I know why it was so hard for me to get attached to a particular person in a romantic way. Because my heart was already taken, and when the heart is taken it cannot be free to love another. It's funny to me that people think that if the abuse finishes, then it is done. But, in a way, that final moment is exactly the moment that everything starts ... that is exactly the moment that the consequences of abuse begin. It is the moment you lose your first love, and it is always said that you never forget your first love. There is something to that ... but what is most distressing is that when one says to me that my response is very subdued and I, in some sense, seem to agree with the statement that I do not believe in love. As a force of habit, I returned to this even with you, saying that I do not really agree. I do not have control over this pattern. Because what I am supposed to say when people tell me that I do not believe in love because I went through incest? What can I say? That my heart was taken? There is a limit to how many people it can contain. And it is also difficult to understand that, on the one hand, I am expected to be a classic victim, so that he automatically becomes a sworn enemy. On the other hand, if I say anything like that, then in their eyes I will have nullified the abuse ... and then I will be forced to explain and I simply don't have the strength for this, and I do not want to. Because this means another foray into an intimate place and revisit the relations between him and me, which the majority of the parts inside me are not really willing to do ... Anyway, how is it possible to give words to this or explain? So, it is just easier to agree that I do not believe in love ... It's pretty sad that they think that way ... Even animals know how to love ... and I know it's a harsh statement. But that's how I feel. Everyone around me is willing to listen as long as it fits their definition of the world. But with incest, it does not fit anyone's natural definition of the world.

7:10
It's really not my fault that my heart was taken, I know that it was twisted love, but that's what happens when you succumb to such a captivity, it is almost inevitable that you will develop feelings ... They forget that he was my first for everything, that all my first experiences were with him. Basically, they do not forget, they just don't want to know. And the abandonment and the loss of him without being able to experience any kind of mourning process or, even, a parting process ... Because of this, I have never felt real love in any relationship, except for my last relationship. Because, up until that last relationship, the Ziv of today was not created. And the other parts of me in my heart and in my soul still were connected to him. Only now, a sort of change is starting within me. And I know there is a change, because I have begun to share with you; it's not a secret anymore. If you have any questions feel free ... and you should have a wonderful morning :) because my heart belonged to him. And I felt that I had to agree so as not to be judged, even with you, but it did not sit right with me in my heart, because you are not like everyone else; you do not judge me ... and I felt that you deserved more. Even when it isn't done on purpose -- sometimes, it takes me a while to gather my courage to talk about it ... which for sure isn't easy, even for me. I feel a slight sense of relief that I shared this with you ...

8:30
Are you OK?

8:35
Yes, I am fine, thanks :) And you? I know that I am writing things to you that are far from simple, and even though I know you can handle them, I still wanted to ask, are you OK?

8:37
I am just worried about you.

8:39

Thanks, it is heartwarming. You know, it's okay, relatively. It is not easy to enter the places that I enter, but it's also liberating. But you know, the process from the beginning, with all its difficulties for me, it's my way to love me ... And you can't expect love to only be nice and beautiful; sometimes, love is painful ... For me, it is more painful. But it is better to have painful love than not have any love at all. It really connects me to the last painting that I made. My only way to experience love was if I hugged myself. And I learned from a young age to hug myself. Even if in the drawing I cross my legs, and yes, I see that I cross my legs; I still leave room for a hug. Paradoxically, this crisscross keeps me from breaking apart ...

13:30[38]

Wow, it took me a long time ... In truth, I started painting in the morning and I didn't connect to the backgrounds that I made. I felt they were not right ... Then, I made this background and it connected exactly to my feelings ... I think that the change in the background symbolizes a transition to another part of the process or to another part of me or both ... This is the first time I can feel a transition in real time. This is very special. This painting symbolizes for me a continuation of what I wrote to you yesterday about love. People always ask me why I keep going back there. As if I have control. And who ever said that I left it, so that I would have to return? I think it connects me exactly to the drawing of the flower being picked and to the

---

38 The same theme arises again -- who is the captor and who is the prisoner? Is it a bird of prey returning to a captor's arm? Or perhaps, she is returning to her history, the only home she had.

painting of the falcon with the little bird. Kind of a process like, first he cut, and then he devoured, and now in this painting I became like him in a sense. I am the bird and the hand is his. And even when she flies "free," the home is him, and she always returns home. The background for me is my soul and it echoes it. I know you probably think: who would choose to return to such a chaotic and painful place? So yes, it is true; it is painful, but it is less chaotic than people think. It is to return to a familiar place, it's back to a stable place for me, even if it sounds strange and unclear. But it is my personal maze and I know where the entrance and where the exit are. Not to mention the fact that I really love this painting ... but I really love it ... I am a pretty bird :)

13:45
Who is the captor and who is the prisoner?

6.5.12

11:30
It is hard for me to look at this picture and I am not quite sure why, but it is really hard for me ... I cannot even write a narrative, I feel angry when I look at it, I don't want to look at it right now.

11:50
There are a number of drawings that can be the framework for this embryonic painting. And I wonder why the anger? Towards whom? The previous painting has both strength and dependence.

12:10
Well, I think I'm ready to write about the painting that made me angry ... I think it angered me that there is something servile in this position ... like the figure is giving up and going back into the maelstrom ... This is one part that upset me ... The second

part is trying to keep something until it almost folds into itself. I feel that she could not protect it. The vortex pulled it away from her. I think that this anger reflects sadness. And last night, I did not sleep due to all the sadness. And you are sure to ask why am I so sad or what made me so sad … I do not know and, for the first time yesterday, I did not even try to understand why. I gave sadness the ability to wash away my anger … You see, I had to give anger this way to express itself … This painting symbolizes a lot of helplessness … because, it is to be in the eye of the storm and there is no place to run … Like the universe took something that belongs to me.

16:45
I think this painting reflects all the processes at once. And beyond that. I love it, because it shows the unbearable fragility of emotional imbalance. And how much sensitivity and tenderness I need to balance myself again. I must search for the exact feather to be able to breathe again.

19:00
Age 14

To feel such pain for something that I feel relieved that it happened, to feel this divide; it is just cruel … I feel great shame. I do not even know where to start. I do not even know if this is connected to the abuse … For now, do not put this in the presentation; I have to think about it … I was raped at age 14; I remember this very vaguely … I know who did it; that's pretty much all I remember. And I think that this rape resulted in a pregnancy … It was not my uncle …

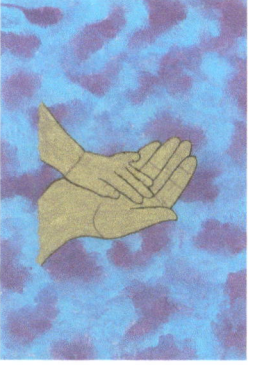

7.5.12

14:50
Today, I was in therapy. Sometimes, after a therapy session like this, I sit down to write to myself. So I'll write here what I have to say. I had a bad feeling today at therapy, to come after so much time, and to drop such a bomb. I did not even know how to start talking, and if I could start talking. I had no idea what I would say. I remember. I remember all the parts surrounding it, but not really what happened there. I remember where it was. I remember who it was. I remember what my brain allows me to remember ... But emotions remember. These are the situations that drive me the craziest, the one where my body and my emotions remember but my brain does not seem to be in sync with them. I have hardly slept at all in the last few nights. I haven't really eaten, and what I do eat I throw up. The body can no longer swallow, which tells me that my emotions can't take it anymore. So all that's left is to curl up into the fetal position and let the whirlwind sweep me off my feet and take me where it may. I'm used to this process; I have been through it many a time, though every time it is just as exhausting and painful. I remember he was older than I was by about 8 years; I was 14. He was an acquaintance, not a friend. We never really spoke except during the time we spent together in our lesson, which was the only hour a week, on a good week, when I could leave the house. It is remarkable; I even forgot I was in a Krav Maga class. I looked for a release for my rage. I was filled with so much rage, and Krav Maga was my place to release some of it. He trained with me, but he also was an instructor. And I remember that we were at a two-day training camp. Wow, what persuasion it took for my mom even to agree to let me go on this trip. What irony ... I swear that this universe has made me into its own private joke. And I remember sleeping outside in sleeping bags. And when he just casually got into my sleeping bag. And this is all I remember. I do not remember what happened inside my sleeping bag. And what does it really matter after everything my uncle had done? What could he have done to make any sort of substantial difference? And I remember that morning came and he was not there. I do not remember what happened until the morning, how long he stayed with me, if he stayed with me. There were two friends of mine there with

me who felt something was wrong. And I think I spoke to them; I do not think I told them exactly what happened, but I remember some sort of general conversation ... If only I could ask them today what it was ... But of course, with me, nothing ever is so simple. Both friends died; one died in an accident in the army at the age of 18 and the other died of a rare brain cancer at age 19. It is weird to have been raped in such an idyllic place. And by someone that I never imagined capable of such an act. I'm so tired and exhausted, and the last thing I needed was something like this. What drives me crazy is that I did not remember it at all. It did not even cross my mind once, so why now? And I do not know if I should even get into this, but it's not the only rape I have been through, so what is the big deal with one more? And yet somehow it is such a big deal that I chose to suppress it completely ... And now I remember what he looked like. I have not seen him in over twenty years and I remember what he looked like. I cannot even remember what my mother looked like, and I can remember him. And the truth is that I have had enough; there are people who look back on their lives with longing for the past, I look back on my life and I fall apart ... And I dare anyone to tell me there is justice in this world. And do not try and tell me that everyone has his burden in life, mine is not a small package, mine is a cargo ship trying not to capsize.

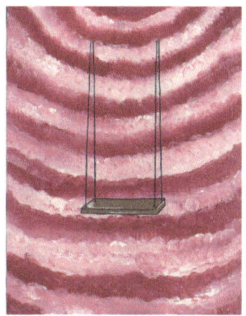

19:00
It may seem like a small painting but the meaning ... it resonates alone ... an orphan swing ...

19:20
And age 14 returns

21:30
I have to ask why do I keep drawing feet and hands? What does

this mean? Can you tell me? I know, you do not want to interfere, but I'm trying to understand and I just can't ... Incidentally, this painting connects me to our conversation today ... I chose to dive in ... The screen starts to rise ...

21:45
As you wrote previously, what caused the experience to become something that needed to be erased? And where does abortion come in? There must have been something there beyond the act itself that was so shocking that you were ready to ignore it and not tell your friends who saw on your face that something had happened.

22:00
I do not think I was ready for it ... It came as a surprise. You see the abuse had become a rooted process, although there were surprises in the beginning. At the age of 14, there were no more surprises; it was part of my existence and that was after a long period of cooperation ... my soul protected me and my brain never referred to it as rape ... make no mistake and do not misunderstand me ... It was rape and it was cruel ... But it had become part of my life and the brain finds it difficult to process persistent rape, so from my perspective, there was this cooperation; it was mutual. It was my way to restore a little control over what happened and was happening to me ... What caused this to be something that had to be erased? I do not know, I can say that intensity of the dissociation was very high. Perhaps, it was caused out of a sense of helplessness, and, perhaps, because this was a situation I could not even begin to deal with ... I had a sick mother at home, I was suffering the abuse, I was alone with myself without anyone ... Maybe I could not deal with this as well and my mind simply shut out this rape ... I do not remember anything unusual about the act itself except that he gagged me so I would not scream and no one would hear me ... but I would not scream at this point, I already knew to keep my mouth shut. I was well versed in that ... It is sad to read that, no? And truthfully, I do not know if there was a pregnancy. I will just write what I remember

and maybe it will clear some things up for me ... Or maybe not ... I do not know if it was his or my uncle's ... But after about two weeks, I was with my uncle. And sometimes, he was somewhat crueler in the act, a bit more dissociative so that he was really not sensitive to me. After this act, I started to bleed, but it was not my period rather something directly caused by the sexual act ... There was bleeding with a lot of pain and I didn't know why it was happening. I associated it with the act ... but it had been a long time since I had bled because of a sexual act. Perhaps fear convinced me to think it was because of the act ... Maybe it really was the act ... That's what I remember which is why I said it was just a feeling, although something inside tells me that this feeling is right, but I just do not know ... Maybe I should rely on emotion more than on reason and the emotion feels like heavy grief ... I did not tell my friends out of shame. What exactly was I going to tell them? Especially since I was already used to keeping quiet ... you draw it all inside until it's gone ... and then you can see it disappear completely ... I try to look at it from the outside like you said, like a movie that isn't happening to me right now ... It's really hard, but it is what needs to be done so I will close my eyes and start ... And therefore, I speak in plural ... Because it is the present day me, and her ... I feel she takes me by the hand and draws me in ... As you said, it did not happen today, but, in her perspective, it happens today ...

8.5.12

4:00

Rachel, it was more than two weeks after the rape. Sorry, time is a bit of a problematic subject ... But I shared with my uncle what had happened. I remember that the sexual act was aggressive, because I told him what had happened. He was caught up in a fit of fury and took it out on me ... This caused a deep understanding for me. We always are talking about the need to control, but it is more than that; it is a fit of rage with sexual expression. The most surreal thing was that he said perverts like that should be murdered. I do not know if I should laugh or cry; someone needs to tell me how to respond, because I have no idea what to do. You do understand that according to my uncle, my attacker did not do the same thing, rather something much, much worse and cruel. The most astounding thing is that, at that moment, I loved him for protecting me like that. It is absolutely crazy.

4:10
This rage came from a place of jealousy regarding his private property. Your feeling is very understandable. Or perhaps, this rape was so significant and pushed out of your mind, because there was an element of betrayal, an element that anything goes, an element of reading you and your life experience, although nothing was spoken. And, in addition, there was something so shocking, otherwise it would not have been deleted from your consciousness and referenced so many times in your paintings. Perhaps, you have similar subconscious feelings toward the abortion.

4:30
It might sound strange, but I understand his rage. The time and effort he expended to control me and to make me his property all those years … it was all taken from him in several hours … But yes, what you wrote is true … I'll tell you something, they always talk about Freyd's betrayal trauma theory … And about all the things that betrayed me, and everyone who betrayed me -- he betrayed me, my family, society, my body and my emotions … but my guilt actually is my betrayal to everyone. You understand, they locked me into the victim role and it overrode all my human experience … According to everyone else, I did not betray, I couldn't, because I was the victim and the victim is betrayed and not a betrayer … This is a correct statement, but not in the context of incest. You understand, they even canceled out my guilt, but my guilt is also my inner compass to what is right and wrong … For most children, it is their parents, society is the compass that teaches them what is right and wrong. I did not have and do not have this compass. My compass is internal not external and part of it is this guilt … But when you grow up so does your guilt. It does not stay the same as it was when you were a child or even an adolescent. Guilt becomes a tool for conduct and it protects your soul. You see, guilt is part of my system to maintain my own identity separate from his. And not only this, but the guilt also cancels play and imagination. Why? Because my imagination was not like all the normative children's imaginations? Or because the games were different? I also was a child, but I played differently and

imagined differently. Believe me, when dissociating, the imagination works overtime. And again, all the theories strip me of the human experience. Why? Because it is OK to cancel out the victim when you are trying to "save" him ... You know, I read quite a few articles, and most of them talk about the emotional absence, the physical absence. There is no cancellation. Rachel, it is not correct ... I was a child, but a different type of child ... If a normative child expresses his childhood as dictated by social constructs, then I expressed my childhood as he dictated. But it was a different, more mature childhood ... You understand, they are canceling out my childhood ... I remember he played children's games with me, not only adult ones ... Chutes and Ladders, Hide-and-Seek, cards, checkers, everything. But it was with him and almost always only with him, and sometimes with my mother, she was sick and this was part of the time that we spent together. It is true that it was not normative ... But you know something, this limited group outside myself allowed me to expand my inner self and I do not regret it ... I have an inner world that is wide and deep, and it is enough for me. How many people can say that they are enough for themselves? How many people can say, "I am not afraid to be alone?" So yes, I'd rather be alone than with others ... and it goes against the general grain of things. So what? So I'm different; being different does not mean that I was not a child in my way or his way ... It does not matter. In the end, I was a child ... Wow, look where I ended up. It is not at all what I intended to write you, and now I do not remember what I wanted to write! ! ! ! ! Do you understand now what happens to me when I am writing? ? ? ? ? I'll try to remember and I will send you the picture I am working on now. Sorry.

5:50
Guilt, Ziv, is a way to preserve a sense of control. If I am guilty, I could, therefore, have done things differently. Guilt allows preservation of the status quo. If in any case I feel bad about what I did, and that is my punishment, I can continue down the same road. There is no need to change. There is a difference between guilt and responsibility. You are not responsible for what happened. The person who is responsible is the person who had the power and the resources. The responsibility always falls on the adult. The adult's responsibility includes the way he reacts to events, memories, and experiences related to childhood and adult-

hood. You do this constantly, dealing with the parts that you think that you should not be allowed to express themselves despite their presence within you.

12:00
This painting reminds me of the painting with the cage. I'm trying to think of something he could do to me that was so shocking that it made me lose all memory of it ... You know, I remember the rape that happened afterwards was especially violent ... But I remember it ... So why the hell do I not remember this? You know, during the rape that happened afterwards, he split my head open, he beat me severely, he raped me for hours ... I have a scar on my forehead that reminds me of it every day ... That's why I almost never look in the mirror ... and still I cannot remember. It is so frustrating! I think I wrote to you before from a place of a lot of frustration ... By the way, I agree with everything you wrote. Do not look at what I've written as something that discredits what you wrote, but rather adds to it ... Wow, you are the only one I told about the rape aside from my therapist. I usually say I do not remember ... Because, who wants to remember this kind of pain and humiliation ... And the craziest thing is that while he beat and raped me, he told me in the same breath he loved me ... I am flooded ... I did not even process one rape and now another one ... and as it turns out, it was probably worse ...

12:30
Age 14 comes up again. What do you see when the picture is upside down?

12:35[39]
When I turn over the painting, I feel that it is a painting of

---

39 Upside-down, it is clearly visible that a figure of a girl is being poured out of the pitcher along with white material, resulting in a sort of black spider. Her hands and feet are shackled.

release ... As if I am released from prison only to find out that I am also chained on the outside ... It is this circular captivity, until I find a way to free myself, I find that after liberation I basically remain bound ... It's like a safe inside another safe ... I think that it is more than my usual frustration today ... That until I find the courage to free myself, until I can find the key, then I find out that I have to find another key ... Like a treasure hunt  just to find out that it leads to another one ... It feels like a journey within a journey within a journey ... And journey with so much equipment on my back which is exhausting enough ... It reminds me of the painting with the scale, the feeling that a tiny feather is enough to shake me emotionally, mentally and physically ...

9.5.12

5:00
My uncle was very aggressive with me, but never hit me ... I'm talking about a rape that happened at the age of 17-18. It was someone else ... You understand, everyone loved me and raped me ... In the context of rape when I was 14 - I can say that I had a feeling I was a whore.

This is a permissible approach for everything ... My feeling was that he just came and took, because I'm a whore ... A tough statement, but that's what I felt. My uncle would tell me this a lot. There was a great sense of confusion and helplessness. My automatic reaction was to disconnect and not fight ... Maybe my uncle's reaction affected me ... That although he was angry at him, my rapist, when he himself was with me in that way, he would tell me regularly that I was a whore ... Maybe he did not notice what came out of his mouth when he was enraged ... It is engraved within me ...

6:00
Rachel,
I know it probably will not be included in the book, but it is

important for me to write it. It took me a while to understand what I write now. We talked about identity and the socialization processes. In fact, my behavior is derived from abuse. I know some of my injuries occurred, because the abusers picked up on me. You know, there is the statement that not all victims harm, but that all abusers were abused ... I agree with this statement. I can sense another victim just from an interaction with them. This is how my abusers picked up on me, because they too were victims ... And you need to be one to identify one ... I do not justify the injustices done, absolutely not, but this understanding helps me calm the anger. I wrote quite a bit about my absorption of his identity, that I am very similar to him in some respects. I also had a few moments that I felt that if I took advantage of a guy, then I could recover my control. Some would call this restoration. I do not know how to perceive restoration, but I want to share with you what I feel. The result of restoration is self-harm. But as soon as it happened, the meaning I gave it was different. You see, the second I take advantage of the moment, it is I who is raping the one who is with me ... It did not happen a lot, but it did happen. It is a different type of restoration than people think ... I behaved the way he behaved towards me knowingly or unknowingly ... I copied him ... I felt a lack of control and wanted control. In my experience, I'm the one who got hurt. The meaning I gave to this moment is important, not the result. Because at the root of this exploitation, I actually was, for a few moments, him ... I have experienced lack of control and I felt the need to regain control in a sexual way. I walked around with a constant pornographic film playing in my head. It is difficult to control such a basic instinct when it is continuously played in your head ... So this is a way to restore control. I guess that they too are walking around with pornographic films in their heads and this is their way to get control. Maybe they have learned the same thing that he taught me, that anger is unloaded through sex. I'm no longer in this place. They are not sick, they just have not learned anything different ... Maybe they are captive, just like me, but they are in a captivity of aggression. The only way for them to regain control of their masculinity. I think the process I am going through allows me to see things in a much broader sense and not divide the world into victim and aggressor ... Life is so much easier when people are categorized into groups ... I think that the process took that from me. On the other hand, the advantage of the present process is that I find myself seeing the world in more broad terms ... I will not forgive him for what he did to me. I do not think I need to forgive. I was hurt and I pay a price for it. But I also need to understand them, the offenders, it calms my anger. If not me, then who knows how hard it is to fight against an identity embedded in you since childhood? I am lucky; that's how I feel. I had and have the supernatural power not to give in ... I do not justify those who surrendered but I can understand them.

6:30
I read the two sections. I was confused by the request to not get angry about the passages you sent me to be read. I am not really sure why you think I would be angry, for what exactly? What did you want to tell me that you did not say? When you talk about abusers and exploitation, where does it exist in a meeting between us?

6:45
Because I have a hard time with what I wrote ... I don't know, what I wrote defies common sense and goes slightly against the mainstream ... So I'm always careful ... It for sure does not happen in our meetings. That's why I took the liberty to write to you what I wrote. Specifically with you, I really do not feel it ... I'm quite comfortable with you, I like it ... With you I feel genuine reciprocity! But every time I expressed some empathy or understanding even if it is in a very limited sense to abusers, I have been attacked. This is the first time that I am writing what I feel, and I probably transferred my burden on to you ... Maybe, I am not sure ... It's really not at all about our relationship. I must say that I have never felt so comfortable with someone who allows me to say things that I never had the courage to say. However, I would really have liked a response to the second section. The section that I sent you about the abusers was necessary for a release ... That's all. The second section is more important to me ... Do you have any questions or comments?

7:50
Rachel, it is important for me that you know and understand. I

am writing to you things that I do not dare to say to anyone else. I trust you ... I know that sometimes it seems that I am testing you or trying to send a message. I'm not trying to test you or to send you subliminal messages. If I have something to tell you, I'll say it outright. I feel safe enough with you and with myself. And I am not writing this in anger, even if it seems that way. It is exactly the opposite. It was written with a lot of positive emotion. I really let myself open up to you. I'll go with you where you lead and not with my eyes closed, but with the feeling that I'm going through a process that I must go through. I trust you! I usually do not trust others, and I am surprised that this trust feels right and safe; I do not try to fight it. I go with the flow ... I am just careful, because, in the past, I received responses that were less than empathetic. This is why I called you, not because I really thought you would get angry, you know, if I really thought you would be angry with me, I would not have written what I wrote. But because I have experienced severe reactions from others for much more trivial things. My automatic response is to warn before ... This is my issue, not yours and it is not about you ... Rachel, I chose to go through the process with you. If I had doubts, I would not open to you like this ... Believe me. And, while we are on the topic, I would like to take this opportunity to say thank you for letting me choose you :)

10.5.12

8:45
I sent you two different angles of the picture from above and from the angle I see it. This painting scares me, it makes me nervous, I do not know why but I am feeling very ill at ease. There is a sense of instability in both me and my body ... And now I realize that I separate myself from my body ... It is strange. I am so attached to it I don't know why I wrote what I wrote. And actually I used metallic colors, ones that are  soothing, and look what came out! This is one of those times

that I feel that it is not I who paints, but rather part of me is trying to say something. This painting does not come from a conscious place ... And maybe that's what scares me ... There is something terrifying in it. Or maybe it's just my feeling, I don't know ... Can you tell me how you feel about the painting? Only if it's okay ... And I have a small addendum to what I wrote in the previous email ... The question of whether I want to tell you something. So after I let go of everything that was in my stomach, I took a deep breath and thought about it ... So I wanted to tell you this: I think you are a special person, and you bring out the special qualities in me and I think the feeling is mutual ...

13:00

I drew this now. I said I would ignore it, but I had to let out what I am feeling ... You know what I realized? It amazes me. Each painting does not belong to one cycle, but rather it is part of several cycles. This needs to be in the book, so people will understand how complicated it is and how each cycle connects to other cycles. There is nothing that stands alone; things always depend on other parts. I drew the first tree as if it is covered by fog, the second tree begins its ascent and the fog begins to fade, and this tree is naked and you can see how it branches out and how each part is connected to the other ... This is what's behind the fog ... It's at once scary and wonderful.

13:50

And again age 6 comes up. Within this number, we see the branching out of branches.

Look at all the trees you have drawn up until today from this vantage point, what do you see?[40]

---

40 You can see significant differences between the first two drawings and the third black tree. The upturned trees where the top and roots can appear from any angle represent the lack of change in time. Although it has truncated branches, no leaves, no glamour, and has an altogether depressing feel, the black tree indicates the beginning of change.

When Time Stood Still

14:30

I see: an emotional process - In the first picture, there are lots of colors with no real focus on any specific one, lots of mixed-up feelings with a sense that the tree is full and cannot accommodate more, therefore it spreads in all directions. In the second picture, the projection of the emotions is more focused. They are focused on the tree and its surroundings, but background is very pastoral. The third picture - the emotions are more controlled; they are no longer on the tree and the surroundings, they are just in the apple - it is symbolic that from an emotional chaos a more conscious, more controlled feeling has emerged. There is my process with him - at first, I saw him as a tree filled with lots of power which includes all colors. In the second picture, he started to lose power in my eyes. He started to fall and his colors are not the entire universe anymore, just a part of it. And in the third picture, he is already naked in front of me, his colors have faded, and all the colors that were in him are now passed on to me. The girl has undergone a process - the first picture is the girl, emotional, impulsive, and entirely filled with pain. In the second picture, the girl is more restrained and she no longer completely fills me. She moves along the site of the tree. And in the third picture, the girl is much more relaxed. She trusts me more. She allows herself to trust me. The colors symbolize an emotional rest. And then there is my process - the first picture was full of fog, I couldn't see the tree and what it contained. In the second picture, I could start to look inside but slowly and assuredly, because the leaves had just begun to fall away. In the third picture, I can see the tree clearly and what is in it. And there is the movement - in the first picture, there is upward movement, unilaterally. In the second picture, the movement is bilateral, and in the third picture, the movement stops.

11.5.12

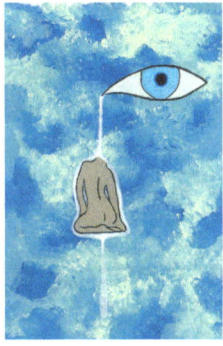

2:20
I think it's an amazing picture. I did not plan for it to come out so special ... I wonder if we see the same thing ... This is not a test, just curiosity. :) Because I feel we are so in sync, that it just interests me. This picture reflects what I wrote to you in the previous email. I feel like my emotions are dripping out of my eyes into the outside world. I painted this picture with so much sadness. I am writing you this email with tears streaming down my face, almost like in the picture. You know, I am told I should cry all the time. There are those who think I don't cry. I was crying inside for so many years until I was filled up inside with tears, and now there is no more space inside and so I step outside myself. And I know that the vacated space inside will quickly become filled with other tears, with other pain ... I have no room inside for all the pain. I constantly have to make room for it. During my childhood, I made room by using dissociation, today I turn to treatment. And it's exhausting that the dissociation no longer exists to eliminate situations, because I deliberately choose not to use it anymore. Today, I use dissociation just to give myself some air in between, to not crash. And this choice brings all the dissociations to the surface and they float in my eyes until the situation decides to spill out into the world.

4:50
In the picture, I see a face without a mouth ... I did not mean for it to come out this way, but the body has become a nose. This is what I see in the picture ... I think that's the feeling I have when I need to talk about the language and the discourse that was going on there. And yes, I was his princess, but a princess in a cage ...

The thing is he did not put me in the cage and watch me from outside of it. He was with me in the cage ... I have a sort of feeling that he did not create the cage just for me. He shared his cage with me and locked me away with him. I think it's a continuation of the picture that I painted with the cage; it really connects me to him. Only this time, I'm trapped inside a tear. Maybe because I understand more, because I am more aware. Perhaps, because I feel more sadness than anger. Maybe because when he left and took me out of this shared cage I created another cage just for me. It took me time to learn that my cage had a key ... Maybe the time I spent inside is what hurts me. And maybe I had already created the cage around myself when I was still with him in his, and I was inside two cages and didn't even notice ... And the second seems more fitting to me ... Because with him there was one type of behavior, and by myself, I behave entirely differently ... And how depressing is that when you leave his cage just to surround yourself with another cage that you built yourself?!

15:15
This is the first time I have painted with watercolors. I call this picture "My Flower Trail." :)

15:20
How old was your mother when she passed away?

15:21
47

15:24
Your father, how old was he?

50-51. Why?

15:25
There are 53-54 flowers along the trail[41]

15:26
:) This to me is what I am creating from now on. This is my own path void of anyone else's shadow.

12.5.12

18:45
This is my constant state ... To enter or not to enter ... I must tell you that I do not often encounter situations that make me cry ... Anger occasionally causes tears, but every time I paint a significant picture, even if it is a simple one, I just feel myself choked up with tears which then pour out of me ... And it is different because it is subtle, but I can still feel the emotion ... There is something in illustrating the emotion that allows me to experience a subtlety that I hadn't yet ... You know, all my life I have experienced violence and physical, mental, and verbal aggression, and drawing gives me the opportunity to connect with myself in a different way ... Am I explaining myself properly? I really hope so ... But this feeling is liberating, and it is strange, because I feel tremendous pain when I paint, but I do not care, and I do not even know why I do not care ... I am experiencing a different kind of pain, an especially nonviolent pain, nonviolent to the body ... There are moments when I am holding the brush, this is what I feel ... Afterwards,

---

41 The semen stains from a previous sketch have become flowers. In a therapeutic process known as REFRAMING non-positive factors or experiences are given a positive use. Recycling of waste (or alternatively pain) for different, useful purposes.

the familiar pain returns, but knowing that I can experience a different kind of pain ... This is a new experience for me ... This is why I paint without stopping, the new kind of pain; it allows me to enter places that I did not dare to enter before ... To reveal things that I thought I would never disclose ... And although you probably see things I do not even come close to seeing, I still feel them ... It is an interesting and intriguing combination ... It might sound strange, but I draw very gently. I feel as though I'm stroking the canvas ... And it's nice. It is amazing that I can make a reparative experience for my body through painting ... Who would have thought? And you should know, I meant to write something completely different, but this is what came out. Sometimes it's frustrating, but I'm going with the flow.

22:10
When I write or talk, second or third person narratives distance me from the experience. This is a very subtle form of dissociation. I cannot always deal with the words or with what I see, even in the drawings. When I think about it and pictures float up into my memory, then they are locked up in my head. When I let them out, then it gives validity to what I have in my mind. Then I cannot cope, especially the first few times; it takes time until I  understand and accept that the experience has been let out of me. It's a place with a lot of shame and guilt and anger and pain, and my automatic reaction is to be present and not to be present. Besides, when I talk about it in the first person, I experience it again in those moments ... And when I talk about it from the outside, I'm more focused ... You will see fragmented parts which mean that there are times when the past is fragmented from the present and therefore the speech becomes fragmented as well ... It is clear to me that I went through everything, but the way I talk shows my inner experience and that I am fragmented into pieces ... That each shard is a different experience and feels dif-

ferent ... When I wrote what I sent you, it was just the beginning of my writings and it was very hard for me, it was the first time I really let out what was in there ... And the words hurt me, physically, they hurt so that I had to keep them away from me in order to cope and to continue ... This writing is depressing and blunt and painful, it is very difficult to be present without disconnecting, and I also need time to process and understand ... The things are in my head, they have no validity until they come out of me ... It seems to me that my writing is coming out messy ... What I'm trying to say, in a very roundabout way, is that I have very little control over what I say, or write, since the use of second or third person narrative is the result of an emotional state.

13.5.12

21:05
Lips came up in one of the very first paintings, detached from the face. The puzzle that makes up the lips is made of very small pieces but they are all connected in one frame. It points to age 36-37, the age you are today, no?[42]

21:15
Yes, I am 36 and a half.

21:17
So the puzzle becomes whole?

21:20
I think so, 36 years I lived in a bubble and in silence, and some

---

42 The six dark pieces of the puzzle represent age 6, the age when the abuse started.

thing changed. I allow myself to write, to draw, to say things I would not dare say. It is not simple at all, to be silenced for so many years and then to find your voice ... It took me many years of therapy to even begin to search for it, my voice. Finding my voice was an almost impossible task, luckily it was only nearly impossible. This process made me realize how many parts inside me need to change ... How many of my parts follow his pattern, I thought they were my own, but I find that many of them belonged to him and they have found their way into me ... The difficult task is to discover which patterns ... Change is like a house of cards, caution should accompany change ... In short, I'm cycling within myself ... and have been doing these spirals for more than six years.

22:00
Sometimes there simply are no words ... To talk is to leave my cage, it is not simple to leave it, and it is not simply sharing what is inside it ... And when I speak, sometimes I need to disconnect myself in order to deal with my exit from the cage and to allow someone else to enter and see the experiences it contains ... This is the most intimate and personal part of me ... I spent years inside of it and it feels like an intrusion ... But it feels this way only for certain parts inside me, nowadays, I am very happy that someone is willing to follow me into the cage and see this captivity ... And yet it fluctuates from dissociation and silence to speech and presence. Between being me and not being present at all ... It hurts to talk about what happened, it hurts to know I went through it, a great sense of shame wraps around me ... Look at what I wrote! Using these words when I talk about myself, it's hell ... Especially since I come from a family where this kind of language is absolutely frowned upon. Forget what happened, it does not exist in the lexicon, I'm talking about words, not actions. If my mother was reading this, she would kill me just for using this language ... But that's what happened and there is no other language to describe it. You can't make something so outrageous into something beautiful just through the use of language ... The truth is shocking and the language should reflect that ... That's why I have to occasionally disconnect myself and then return ... Not to mention that he spoke in first, second and third person, it is another thing I learned from him ... Even

when he was explaining things to me, he often referred to me in the second person. So, it was internalized ... I started talking to myself the same way ... It was easy, because it was as if I was not there ... This made it easier, because if I talked to myself in the second and third person when I was with him then it was as if I was not there ... It created a separation between me and the girl in his eyes. I'm sure that he disconnected from the fact that I was a child, and my speaking in the second and third person erased in a certain sense my presence in front of him. In addition, for me, personally, it deleted my presence entirely ... As it was, I did not feel an identity in the physical world, and the language used then and now transported my inner experience. And today the use of second and third person allows me to do exactly what it allowed him to do, to disconnect and make a separation between me and the girl ... I did not see it, I started writing and it just came out ... This is very interesting and new to me.

22:30
Do you know what I discovered now? I have to share it with you. Every time I get some insight relating to him and the connection to his identity within me, I dissociate ... Now, I am disconnected, and I know that I am ... It is as if my insight finds balance, and then I disconnect, because it is hard for me to retain the knowledge because I have so many parts that do not belong to me. It is hard for me to accept it, so I disconnect ... But it is not a run-of-the-mill disconnect in order to brush something off, it is a detachment in order to return to equilibrium ... This prevents the insight from totally flooding me, thus, there is almost no emotion, just everything trying to restore order in the disturbance ... Wow, how many different types of disconnections can there be? It is exhausting ... That's why I am not painting now, because I cannot connect to my feelings ... You asked me once when I took a break from painting why I stopped ... So it took me a while to figure things out, but I will tell you about it now ... In general, the painting that I am doing and the process that I am undergoing with the treatment makes me understand things through emotion and not only intellect ... and I usually had intellectual understanding in the past ... So this depth brings parts to the surface that I was not aware of, parts that I am living with, parts that run my life ... And I never would have guessed that it

was not mine at all. It's his. When you asked where he ends and I begin, then there apparently is no beginning and end ... because I do not see and I do not feel neither a beginning nor an end ... And since painting brings out my suppressed parts, my spirit needs breaks in order to handle a cluster of pictures, or to complete a cycle of pictures, before it begins another cycle ... And each cycle brings up other parts. And I know I have not finished with age 14, but maybe it will come out in the next cycle.

14.5.12

7:15
They keep telling me to leave the abuse behind. I wish I could! They just don't realize that it is even in the simplest of places ... even food ... yes, also in food ... Every time I feel flooded, I eat what he made or bought me after he was with me. And every time I eat this food, I go back to that place, or I am returning from that place ... And it's not that they are special foods, they are everyday foods ... How can I explain in words that abuse is an integral part of me? It is hard for me to process, so I guess it would be intolerable for others ... I remember he used to prepare food for me based on my behavior and according to his mood. Wow, that sounds terrible, but you get used to it ... If I was a really good girl, then he would put a lot of time and effort into preparing me something sweet or he would buy me something delicious ... If I was not as good, he would prepare me something small, just to make me something, or he would buy me food that didn't even enter into the equation ... I think this was his way of showing me that he was disappointed or angry. Food plays a significant role in my life, even though I never had an eating disorder as it would be clinically defined ... But yes, the food I eat relates to my state of mind and how I feel ... But what makes me angry is that I eat the same things he ate; the main components of my food choices are the same as his. It's frustrating that everything reminds me of him. It's frustrating that it comes in the smallest and most everyday things. It's frustrating, because it is nearly impossible to change my taste in food at this point, and it is something that will always remind me of him ... And what is most frustrating is that I revolve around him so much, whether I want to or not. And I have no control over it, because it's not something you can control. I grew up with

it ... Tastes, smells, touch ... How can I change everything? I also do not want to ... Ultimately, it is to remain trapped forever, with enough of a margin to live, but that's all ... It will sound strange to you, but there are things I prepare to this day just like him ... Not that I want to, it has just become automatic ... I think this is the part that misses him and keeps him in my life with food and taste ... Sometimes, when I'm in a bad mental state and I want to buy what he used to buy, I fight it, this isn't just a statement rather an actual battle with myself not to buy it ... Sometimes I speak with Miri and she manages to make this need go away. Not always, but sometimes she can ... That's strange, because when she can, or when I can hold out and not revert to the familiar, comfort food ... And it is certainly a metaphor ... That it is actually about going somewhere familiar, to him ... I can talk more about the things, since that need is not satisfied. And it's not a simple act, because when I deny myself this need I am filled with rage ... It is abated fairly quickly, but still ...

9:20
Something in me feels really restless ... Classical conditioning. Is there a way to miss something via food? I do not know, but it feels that way ... There's a song by Keren Peles, "She Ran Home." I listened to it a lot recently and it is very similar to how I feel sometimes ... I really love it, the song has amazing meaning.

It happened like that, you had no choice
Just to pull the trigger, close the crack
That noise didn't do it for you
Preferring the quiet, feeling paralyzed
Not yours, and how he loved you
This is how you laugh, small and suppressed
Throwing it all, there was nowhere left to fall
Because you were already down, already down ...
You race home
Ongoing madness,
To lose yourself at his feet
You race home,
To return yourself to yourself from his breath
You race home,
The known warmth from another day is alienated

Home home,
On your silence that keeps you...

So then, you're addicted
To his open body, come and relax like a bright thunder,
He tries to hide in his voice that is calling you
What is missing in you,
Anyway, this is a confused world,
Exploding everywhere, covered in lies
Easy to browse, to slightly lose your head
So you sailed, and sailed...
You race home...
No lights, just covered walkways
Fog clears to forgive,
No memory, only the last flicker
Trying to hold you by force
There is no love, only extinguished habit,
So do not give him your heart to trust
No guilt, only a wall!
Shatter! Break! Breach! Crack! By Force!

10:30
Yesterday, I was disconnected and today, somehow, my rage has started up... At least now I'm more connected to this cycle... It is more organized in my head... At least rage does not surprise me, only this time it's a different cycle... I did not understand why I decided to write to you about food yesterday. It was like it came out of nowhere to change the subject and the sequence... And suddenly I realized yesterday that I was really in the mood for pizza, but I stopped myself. And in the cycle there is an emotional flooding, dissociation, and then comes the desire to eat something that is somewhat connected to it... Food comforts me, and if I deny myself this food, then anger follows because I have effectively denied myself comfort. Relief only comes after the anger has been vented. Here is something that I have not shared, or at least I think I have not shared it with you, there is another variable that exists in this cycle... sexuality. Food does not break the rage, it simply compresses it deep inside and comforts me in the short term, out of grace. Sex, however, breaks apart the anger inside of me. Not that I'm doing anything in

this regard ... That's why I have these kinds of fits from time to time. Before this I will tell you that he consistently used to let out his rage, inside me. And I think that as a child, I absorbed his immense amounts of rage until there was no place left inside me for my own. Then I started to unload my rage with him. And that I what I learned, that through sex you can unload harsh feelings. And when rage rears its head nowadays, I automatically am sent to that familiar place, and since I do not act automatically, rather it is only in my mind and emotions and my body ... The anger grows ... I walk around with a real need to vent without actually acting upon this need ... And I refrain from eating comfort food, so even that small comfort that I know so well doesn't exist ... It is very difficult ... For years, I was, how did Miri put it, the vessel for his rage. I cannot find a better word ... So I have his rage inside me and my own rage as well and I have not even begun to approach his part of the rage. I am still just in mine ... And this vessel is overflowing ... So at the least the cycle for me is flooding, dissociation, food, sex, and then rage ... Then a return to balance (even though my balance is partly dissociative). Then flooding again ... And so on ... And I do not know how to break this cycle. For now, I don't break it, I simply ignore it, or rather I suspend it ... And I am still remembering things ... So that I cannot even delve into or focus more on this cycle ... And how to break it completely ... It sometimes happens that the cycle is flipped due to a sexual stimulation. Then, I turn to food, and if that doesn't come then the anger arrives ... Then dissociation comes, because I cannot deal with both anger and stimulation ... And the stimulus comes, because I remember things, or rather they are constantly there, and then more memories are added ... It isn't easy, but I deal with it ...

15.5.12

4:30

The goal is not to leave the abuse behind you and there is no way to do that. As you said, it's part of your identity, part of your history, part of your childhood. In parallel with the abuse, there were experiences of acceptance and love, and therefore you cannot separate them. There is, however, the possibility to look at everything from an adult's vantage point. Zahavit and Ziv both as one. The puzzle is the union of all the parts, darker, brighter, assembling them all together to one whole. The whole is always different from its parts, remember? But you always can look at each part separately. To be separate and together.

5:10
Do you know what the saddest part is? I know I am doing to the girl what he did to her ... That's why she keeps screaming ... But this time I defend myself and am not unloading things onto her ... But I also do not allow her to vent ... I took everything that was familiar away from her ...

10:20
This is the room that I have inside ...

10:25
This is the room that you are inside or that is inside of you?

10:30
Both. This room, not exactly but very similar. And you certainly are asking, where is he? So, he is the floor which swallows me ... from inside and outside ... I would look at this window for hours. "Look" isn't the right word; I would stare for hours through this window ... The blue symbolizes God for me, even he could not contain this horror, so he stayed outside ... Or is he just watching a movie?

12:00
In a face-to-face meeting, we talked about the meaning of change and the meaning of meeting with the abuser.

14:30
For a brief moment, I had the courage to call him and arrange a meeting time. My heart was beating so fast that I felt like any

minute it was going to leap out of my chest and lay beating on the floor. The process I went through, especially with painting, showed me in no uncertain terms that I am a prisoner. I do not want to be trapped, but I am a captive ... And worse than that I am a prisoner in his cage and my cage, I am captured in two dimensions ... And I was afraid to release him, because who am I without him? In a way, he gave me an identity not only in childhood, but also now ... And I have come to the conclusion that I need to release myself from him. It is strange; after this phone call, I feel so many things. Fear, general hysteria, the need to throw up, that my legs are completely paralyzed, and, finally, relief that I managed to take this step. I hope that fear will not cause me to regret this decision and that I will actually go through with it. But when I am already doing something, I usually follow through with it to the end ... Well, I truly am in a general state of hysteria. My body is shaking uncontrollably ... And I do not even want to ask him anything. I just want to let him know that I know and I remember and it is no longer a secret. It is important for me to let him know that it is no longer a secret. Why? Because the secret is part of the captivity and if I can shatter this part, then the wall is breached and all the parts will fall out and I can get out. I know that seeing him today will be a hard blow to my experience and feelings, but today I am who I am because of me, and I can stand tall facing him. And although in the book no one will know it is him, I will know that it is him and he will know as well ... That's what I want ... I no longer have the need for him to validate what happened. I have no desire for him to ask for forgiveness. I have no need for any reaction whatsoever from him; I just want him to know that I remember. And I know how he will react; he will say that I wanted it or that he had not done anything ... But that's okay. His words will not hurt me anymore, and he taught me not to listen to the words, but to look into the person's eyes. I think I'll write more later because I'm disappearing now ... And I do not feel anger, I just feel like I am sinking into myself ... And it is frightening. I know that I won't be able to criticize him, that isn't my goal ... Just to look into his eyes like he used to look into mine and see everything; this time it is my turn to see everything ... I worked very hard and practiced a lot for this moment ... I wanted to come from a place of strength and safety, not from a fragile, emotional one ...

To verbally barrage someone is to be weak and attack them. I am not going to attack, I'll show him that I'm better than him and he didn't succeed in making me into him!

16:30
I think I know what I want from this meeting. I want to see him as he is today, and to let go of the image I have kept in my mind. I think it will make things a lot easier for me, especially in the scenes played out in my head ... I will see him as he is ... And if I can moderate the scenes in my head, I can curb the dissociation, and therefore I can temper the rage ... This is the goal. It is rational, but at its base, it is completely emotional. I do not even have to confront him; I just need to see him to know that I am stronger than he is today. I need to see the fear in his eyes. I need a role reversal! This time, I need to see his eyes pleading for compassion, just as I pleaded with him during my childhood ... Yes, I am writing from a place of anger, so what?! I need to give him all my fears and watch him shrinking within them. In an instant, he will become the receptacle for my wrath. And I, unlike him, do not need more than one time to break free ... Yes, there will be fits of rage because of other things, but they will not be because of him ... They will be due to situations ... And I can handle that. I want him to feel for a moment what I felt for years. And you know what? I will succeed! I sank for a moment, but I managed to get myself out of there. This tells me that I can achieve what I want and my goal. And my goal is not to confront, it is to minimize. You see, when you face someone who hurt you, you should not confront him, then you give him the option to minimize and harm you ... No, it will not happen this time! This time I will minimize him. I will make him into what he should have been for all these years, a grain of sand. This time I'll be lightning and I'll beat down on him without mercy, without words, with my eyes. I will cast upon him the shame and guilt. This time I'll be God! For just a moment, I will let a part of him come out, and I'll strike it on its way ... This is poetic justice! As he treated me in childhood, he shut me down with just a glance and buried me inside myself, I'll bury him in himself! And I will use him to do this. How did I not see this until now??? I have his part inside me! And I upgraded it to perfection! Now I understand, it finally hit me that, in fact, every word that will be said is an opportunity for

him to attack, then I'll be in a position to be harmed ... No, this will not happen. I know exactly what I'm going to do ... I know that people think we need to talk and confront with words, but this blow will not be with words, at least not out loud, this is an injury of silence, and I'll attack him with silence.

17:10
I'm really excited. And along with it, your legs and stomach will tremble up until the meeting and possibly even during as well. That too is normal.

17:20
Thanks :)

17:50
True, my stomach and legs, and it seems that there will be a lot more pain and anger and frustration and sense of loss until the meeting ... But I have lived with these emotions for years and my body was attacked for years. I think I'll be able to stand it for a few more days ... And it also will not stop there, it will continue to hurt, but for a moment it will not hurt and this moment is worth all the other ones combined ... I know that you play more than just a small part in all of this ... I've spent a lot of time trying to find the courage to do this ... But I had no purpose and no plan of action ... And I was very, very afraid. But the process with you helped to clarify a lot of things. And you and Miri have successfully drawn out a lot of internal power that I always had but simply did not know how to use. I have a lot of power, Rachel, more than I can even contain. It's funny to say, but I have the same amount of power as pain. It is exactly the same amount ... Because each pain has the power that goes with it ... You can't always see it or feel it, but it is there ... And this process has helped me to see it. You see, in my pictures, I not only saw the emotions ... I also saw the inner strengths that accompany them ... And I saw hope and I saw release ... I saw it all. It is my greatest strength ... I never see only the bad or just the good; I always see them together. And you already know quite a bit of what I went through, so think how much pain and how much power ... But this is more than power, it is force ... And frankly, I'm thrilled. I did not know this would be my response, and I did

not know I would come away from this with such a great insight ... I was always afraid of confrontation, because it was not my way of communication. It was a strange new place and one that was not yet optimized ... But now, I feel confident enough to do it the way that I know, in the way that I have power ... In silence ... This is a huge insight ... I know most people have a need to hear the words. I do not have that need; it was not our form of communication and therefore it cannot exist even now. Words have a lot of strength, but, from experience, there is much more to be found in silence!

16.5.12

10:10
I finished the drawing that I started in the morning :)

This is what I was doodling in school ... Exactly what I was doodling in school ... Every year, all my notebooks were filled with doodles.

10:20
Look at the picture upside down, what do you see?

10:30
So you can see that a path has footsteps, but they have no distinct direction, meaning that it can be coming out of me, or going inside. I can say that the house stands on the edge of the mountain and the

mountain is cracking, so it is in danger of crumbling and coming crashing down. On the other hand, it has an amazing view and the sun is shining ... But it is on the edge of a mountain, alone and closed-off ... And I do not know whether or not there's someone in the house ... My feelings are fluctuating now, not flooding, but there are changes, so that sometimes there is and sometimes there isn't anyone at home ...

11:00
I do not think you are truly seeing everything in the upside-down picture, please take a second look.

And here is what I see: upside-down, there are two pairs of legs, a woman's and a man's. Between the woman's legs, there is a snaking path. The house is a shared part of both of their waists. One of the trees is the continuation of the male body. The second tree is the continuation of the woman's body, but it is mostly covered by the house. This is the first picture in which something is shared which is shown by the closed-off house, but each individual stands alone as well.

Just now I had a chance to read. I was in Tel Aviv and didn't see the emails. I think that although as you wrote it was the model that you doodled throughout your childhood, this addition is different and is applicable to your present and the process you went through as you have written. Which is analogous to the puzzle, which combined the ages of 6 and 36. There are no words in my appraisal.

11:30
I know that to an outsider my actions might seem impulsive, that suddenly out of nowhere I get up and do something. I am the most non-impulsive person out there when it comes to things having to do with my spirit. I take a very measured step, and each of my steps undergoes a long and tedious process. And I have many reasons why I do this. Part of this has nothing to do with him at all. I have not shared it, because I do not want to create some sort of disappointment. Since it is a very complex issue and not simple at all, for me, at least. But I'm 36 years old, and I do not have that much time left to bring a child into this world ... The window is closing slowly. And I would not bring a child into this world, the way I am right now. It is irresponsible and wrong, and with my awareness, it would be a crime to have a child. But if I can achieve the purpose for which I'm going to this meeting, maybe, just maybe, this place will change, and maybe I'll feel differently, maybe I'll decide out of awareness and understanding that I really broke the cycle, and so I should have a child.

You see, the cycle will break with me, and if I can break the cycle now, then I might just be able to create a wholly new cycle. And I have thought about it for a long time, and I know that the cycle only will break after meeting with him. But I also know that my goal is not coming from a place of war, but rather a peaceful one ... When I think about this word that they use all the time, confrontation. It is a fundamentally aggressive and violent word. It seems like the victim or the survivor becomes a sacrifice, as the weak one goes up against the attacker. So I have to ask the question ... Why send them to war if they have no chance of winning? In war, there are no winners, only losers, and they have already been injured so why wound them even more? And if so, in the first place you are giving him the strength, not her. There are many things said about strength and power, but it plays out in the life completely differently. You understand, they are sending her out of rage, to have a confrontation, but, in my eyes, a confrontation is a form of weakness. That's exactly the interaction of the abuse; when emotion absorbs a blow, it attacks. And a person who injures knows very well that the one standing before him attacking him is weaker than he is. It is an unfair fight ... And I know this, because I am exactly the same. You attack a person, because you cannot deal with him. Today, I come from a place of wholeness, I have no need to attack or fight. I have fought enough. Now is the time to make my inner peace. For me, it is no longer the main point, rather it is the means ... Just like I was his means ... This is the role reversal.

13:00
So it is like this, I did not have a simple day yesterday, but not because of me which is what I want to stress, I actually felt a sense of wholeness in what I chose to do. But my girlfriend and Miri started to get stressed out and worried. And I found myself comforting them and trying to explain myself. I have no problem with that, on the contrary, I was flattered that they cared about me that much. Just that at that moment, I had to console myself because this wholeness is not easy for me; I am in a sense releasing him. I have not been without him for 36 years; I feel a different kind of loss than the loss I felt after my abandonment ... And now with them feeling so upset, I had to abbreviate the process that I went through with the trees. :) I think that they

will calm down, but, for sure, they will remain on edge until the meeting is over. Luckily, I have enough confidence to stand behind my decisions. It's not easy, because I have to cast this off me, everything he did to me, and see him as he is ... This is my coping mechanism ... You see, I know that everyone wants to come and support me, it's fun to know that. But it started with me and him, and it will end the same way. It may sound strange to you, but I was thinking a lot about my life and the ways in which I dealt with things, and somehow it all comes down to this moment ... I know that I will succeed, because I have been successful more than once in the past, and it is true that it was not with him, but today I can succeed even with him.

14:00
OK, the meeting - I'm not going to say that the book is about him; that way I will be sure that my aunt will not make the connection even to this place, since she is a battered woman. She is captured within herself; she cannot see anything. She for sure will be shocked, but she will be easy to deal with. He might go into total shock, or he might enter into a dissociative state and distance it from himself, which is the option that is more likely to transpire, because it is unlikely that there will be either verbal or physical conflict for that matter. Just as he used to tell me things in a matter-of-fact way, so I, too, know how to tell them in exactly the same fashion. He might get weak in the knees, but he will not dare to talk or speak. In any case, he is as much a captive of the secret as I am, so he will be very limited and this will limit the reaction itself as well. Because otherwise he will be incriminating himself. He is smart, so he will be careful. Or he will try to cut me off, saying it did not happen. The moment I get up and walk out of there will be the moment I'll have achieved my purpose for which I came, even if it means I only will get to look him in the eyes and go. In my opinion, I will have gotten what I wanted. I'm going to the meeting with a deep understanding that I care only about my experience. I'm not going to please anyone else, and I'm not going to do anything I would not feel whole with ... I am going on what feels right to me ... I know this is a significant step, but it needs to be understood that to me the significance is different. And I'm okay with that. And even if I take pity on him, it is fine with me, because, in every scenario,

even one with pity, I still am more powerful than him. The ideal will be shattered ... I'm not afraid of these feelings, I'm not afraid of mercy, I'm not afraid of empathy, I'm not afraid of fear, I'm not afraid of my reaction and I am not afraid of them and their responses. I am coming from a very calm and very peaceful place; it is a place that is very safe, very focused and very me. I do not come from threatening place and I do not plan to say things that have a threatening tone. On the contrary, my goal is not to overwhelm them so that they or he will feel attacked. The goal is to release me, and I will do this quietly with a lot of emotion ... And it's not because I am trying to protect them, I am really not ... I want to be clear, I am protecting myself, and I learned to defend myself well. And since I know them, I also know what to do ... If, in the worst scenario, it does not go the way I thought it would, I will just get up and leave ... But ... The main goal is to break his ideal, and the secondary goal is to tell him about the book ... If I do not have a fitting opportunity, then I will give up on the secondary goal ... I have priorities ... I come first, everything else around me is second. Moreover, the book does not say explicitly that it is him, so it does not really matter in the end ... What matters to me is my therapeutic process ... That's the end goal.

15:00
The one who is giving you strength is your inner caregiver. She has the capacity to grow and to love all the parts and to be sensitive to the girl who grew up in the shadow. She will be there with you; she will understand and help. Do not push her away. Embrace her.

15:30
I know that everyone is worried about me, but I am worried about myself more than anyone else could :) The anxiety and the panic of those who are around me is making me angry.

15:45
Regardless of the concern, I think it's a significant step. There is a goal with several sub-parts, but it is important to remember that you are not the only one in this scenario. There are other factors that can and may do everything to stimulate other parts inside of you, such as empathy, compassion, sympathy, responsibility. The scene or the script in your head will not necessarily be the one which will actually take place. So

leave yourself room for flexibility and adaptability in response to the events that unfold. The anxiety of those close to you in your environment is a reflection of the anxiety that took place within you over the years. The environment also needs to adjust and prepare for change.

17.5.12

6:30
It's true. I see and I saw last time I looked at the painting, but I didn't really want to see ... I think I was in too much of an upheaval about the meeting that is going to take place between us and I was not prepared for this goodbye. Now it is better ... I see my life, more or less. I see the abuse and I see how the house he created was most of my life, the whole middle, my whole body. But at some point, I chose to leave this house slowly, slowly and start to grow on my own. If for my entire life no one could see me because he hid me, today it is impossible not to see me ... But everyone can see the treetop, and I have no problem with it, because it is beautiful. The treetop always is beautiful and you can see the view from it ... But the foundation of the treetop is this house, and this house is really not much, let's face it. But you know that it's my house, and everyone has their house. More than this, it has been years since he has been in the house. It seems that I really am the one who is still holding on to him, because up until now the house hid me and you couldn't see me, but now that I am starting to grow and reach up taller than the house and you can begin to see me. I can make the separation from him. No, it is not true. I will correct myself - as long as the house hid me, I did not see me, I had to hold on to him in order to feel visible. Now, after a long, integrated, very intensive, psychological therapy process which involved narratives and art, I can say that I have started to see me, so I no longer need him to see me ... which is proper. I said that the paintings made me see me, and most of all, I needed this visibility. Not so others could

When Time Stood Still

see me, but so I could see myself ... You know, this affliction is the lack of visibility, and sometimes you think that if you see the person then you give him a corrective experience. The corrective experience is that he can see himself ... Everything else is pure gain ... A person who cannot see himself cannot see the others who do see him. He just does not see, period.

18.5.12
Following a face-to-face meeting with Rachel

14:30
I have nothing to write about this, yet ... This was done with watercolor pencils ... And the figure is not falling; she is climbing either up or down. But she isn't falling ... It's nice to draw with these pencils. This is my first time using them.

15:00
Look at these two pictures, what do you see?[43]

23.3.12[44] 18.5.12

---

43 In the first drawing, Ziv is part of the injury, wandering within it. In the second, Ziv climbs outside of the sex organ, from the earth forever.
44 The date that each drawing was done is written below it. One can see the change that took place in just two months.

15:05
Put both pictures in front of you. What do you see?

15:15
I put the two of them together and it is really amazing ... Apparently, I need to leave the trauma from where I was hurt ... When I look at it, I see that I fell into the trauma and somehow I managed to survive it ... But to leave it requires me to climb through it again ... And to go through all the trauma again, so I can be free of it. The difference is that during the trauma I went through the entire experience in real time, but, during the process, I went through it all from the outside ... But I was close enough to experience everything all over again, as if it happened in real time. But there was always the knowledge that I was on the outside. And I think the last picture shows that the climb is hard and a massive one, and there is no support, not really, there is no rope. It is like climbing using only your hands and feet, and the entire time you are praying that you do not slip and fall back down. And at some point, my arms and legs were burning with pain, and I continued to climb with my last remaining strength in order to come out on top. The process was no less difficult and painful than the trauma was in real time. From the outside, things often look more awful than they were from the inside. The emotions are more painful and the body is more vulnerable ... The climb becomes a difficult and complex task, because of this. And still, it is my choice to go and climb the trauma in order to create, even if I do not have much time left, but to make my remaining time quiet ... And I think the fits of rage and flooding of emotions happened in moments that were already very difficult for me to climb on this mountain. They were a kind of relaxing break from the climb, as weird as it sounds. They created the downtime that allowed me to continue forward ... And it seems that, today, I am standing before the last big uphill, just a little more climbing and I will have reached the summit, and I have gotten so used to climbing it is hard for me to think about the fact that I will not climb anymore ... But somehow I feel that sitting on this mountain and looking at the scenery will be the contrast I need to the difficulty of giving up the climb. Besides, I'm curious, because I have never experienced liberty. I have experienced freedom but not liberty ... I wonder how it will be ... It

seems to me that it will be easier when I release myself from him in order to release myself from my cage, the one that I created.

17:40
The real hardship for me was to give up the parts within me. I did not know how I would feel without them ... Then I realized that it did not give up anything; it's not a loss, rather it is a union ... It is to internally integrate them ... I read quite a bit of research and I watched quite a few shows. And they are always talking about loss ... It isn't a loss though; it is a connection and assembly of different parts. It is the complete opposite of loss, at least for me ... This understanding has created an incredible sense of relief for me ... I do not feel like I'm losing an identity, but rather creating one ... Because of this, I feel now a much larger sense of peace in respect to the meeting, and the closer the time comes, the more something inside of me relaxes. More than that, I think the little girl inside wanted to see him to release me from him ... She wanted closure, so that she can escape this cycle... But because she was screaming the entire time, I could not help but listen to her and try to understand what she wanted from me ... I'm starting to understand and she is starting to speak softly ... Today I got up and scrubbed down my house. It is completely symbolic, but I want to come back to a clean house after this meeting. I would like to be clean internally and externally ... Because it seems to me that after this meeting, I'll begin to breathe again and I want to breathe in clean air.

17:40
A lot of things are coming to mind right now, so I decided to write them all down, so I won't forget anything ... Although I really should prepare for the meeting ... But you know what? It becomes less and less important with every approaching moment. The very decision itself to make the meeting cured so very many things inside of me. Obviously, I still will go, because I have other goals as well, but ... I will write the feelings and thoughts that arise within me ... Because that is important. We have talked a lot and I wrote quite a bit about addiction. So addiction to him was the most massive, the most critical and most significant. The addiction to him made me addicted to so many things that due to these addictions I did not see pleasure in

doing things. Because when I do it out of this addiction, it is not for pleasure, it is simply to satisfy an urge. But I am beginning to break free of my addiction to him. And when I say addiction, it is something that is expressed in so many ways. This addiction to my feelings towards him, both good and bad, it's an addiction to what he taught me, it's an addiction to his presence in my life and to his figure which accompanies me in my day-to-day life, it's an addiction to the parts of me that are constantly trying to deal with the parts of him that are inside me. This is my addiction to the abuse and to my process dealing with it. Yes, you can become addicted to this, too. Because the cycles that form inside me create these addictions. It is an addiction to his touch, to the attention he provided and to the visibility it afforded me. It is very difficult to give up all these addictions ... It is almost impossible, but only almost. Then I realized that just the decision to meet with him has subdued a lot of these needs. I no longer feel the need for the visibility he afforded me, I do not feel the need for his touch, not in my head and not in my emotions. I do not feel that I must disassemble my parts in order to deal with him. And I do not feel vigilant which is a serious addiction, nor guilt. The guilt is completely gone in all matters pertaining to him. I have other guilt, but that's for the next book :)

18:50
My body has relaxed. It still is in pain, excruciating pain. But it has calmed down. Yes, it is a contradiction. Yet, it isn't a contradiction at all, because the body needs time to relax completely. And now, the process is just the beginning. It is nice, I must say. This is the word that I constantly was looking for, because when they are talking about addiction, this is separate from everything else, and the word is captivity addiction. And somehow the success of unraveling the tangle of captivity also can allow a release from the addiction to it. Awesome ... This is new to me, so I am amazed as I am writing about it ... And it is nice, because I am so focused and I do not digress from the topic at hand. :) But this is more than simply releasing the addiction; it is to break the cycle related to the addiction. And I'm sure that the meeting with him, no matter what the outcome will be, will bring another level to this calm, and for some of the addictions it will even bring about their weaning. Since these addictions use all my senses: hear-

ing, speech, sight, touch, everything works in synchronization in order to satisfy the need. And now, as I told you, I heard him and my brain already has started undergoing an adaptation, so that he is no longer threatening me, and then I automatically start feeling more relaxed. And I'll probably need to go through it with all my senses working together in order to bring about the release. And you know what? I'm ready for it. It does not matter what happens there; I will come out complete, and even more than that, I leave with only my identity ... He will not be part of it anymore. And it's true that he will never disappear completely, and it is true that I still will hurt, I do not deny the fact that there are things that will stay with me until death, and I probably will still have downward falls in my mood, but I am no longer afraid of them ... I went through this abuse twice. I am already experienced and ready for the third time ... When all my parts are united and my identity has been stabilized and the little girl no longer shouts, this will be enough for me ... And when pain comes, I'll deal with it in a better and safer way. But most of all, the addiction part of me will calm down, and then I can live a peaceful life without the fear of needing to satisfy needs, both good and bad ... If you have any questions, feel free to ask them. Maybe it will make things clearer.

19:00

It is fascinating. As I told you on the phone, the truth is that I am speechless. I so appreciate the ability, the way, the courage despite the burden, the willingness to jump into the pool despite the cold, the creativity, and cognitive intelligence and especially the emotional intelligence.

Look back at the narrative of the picture that you drew on 22.3, the one where the small figure is in the sex organ. The narrative was that it was difficult for you to look at and it hurts you all over. The climb also was so difficult and your legs were burning with pain. The journey ended with what it started only in a different place. We saw a change from symbiosis and enmeshment to differentiation and individuation—from a screen that came down and then rose due to pain and came down again due to anxiety and flooding—to a stage without a screen that has the ability to show the actress and the story, from fog to clarity, from darkness to light, from panic to calm. From being still and stuck to feeling alive.

Addiction also is captivity. Have you ever heard of the concept of

Stockholm Syndrome? It is love and addiction for the captor. The lack of differentiation between the victim and attacker allows for survival; it prevents the dissonance that can bring the victim to the point of collapse or death. When the victim perceives himself as part of or an extension of the captor, the suffering becomes seemingly bearable, because it is an integral part of the relationship. With suffering, there always is a beginning, middle, and end. The positive continuation of it allows for hope, life, and a separation and distinction between the difficult parts and those which are more pleasant. In actuality, the prison or cage that is built is such that even when there are physical ways with which to leave it, the bars remain in place but are invisible. The biggest fear is how to survive and whether you can survive in another world, in one where there are no risks or hazards, there is no constant coping with physical and emotional pain. Apparently, the fear is of the "nothing," the "emptiness," the "lack of excitement" and then the "lack of emotion."

As you wrote so beautifully, the meaning of change isn't loss, but the integration of all the parts, including accepting those which are less pleasant, that are even painful at times, and providing more room for the other parts, such as the caregiver inside of you, the one that took care of your mother and can take care of you now, finally, the one who takes responsibility for others and now you, not only in the sense of safekeeping, but in the sense of tenderness.

19.5.12
After the meeting with the abuser

21:00
I am trying to sit down and write, but I have to sleep on things ... Everything is recorded, so nothing will get away from me. I do want to release some of what I feel about my cousin. I must say that it is completely surreal ... He chose me to help him ... I know he chose me, but what am I supposed to do? On one hand, he has not done anything wrong to me and he is in danger. On the other hand, though, he is his son. And I know that at the end I'll be there for him ... I had a very deep conversation with him ... It started when he told me he wanted to be an actor. I asked him why. So he said the game allows you to put on a different mask every night and forget yourself, and when he stands onstage, everyone will look at him. Then I asked him if that was what he was searching for, for someone to see him, and he said,

"Yes," and there was a silence full of pain after these words ... He told me that he can't manage to hold on to a job, he can't concentrate to study, that, in actuality, he feels stuck and he can't enjoy anything, that he is having a tough time at home and spends most of the day closed up in his room (sound familiar?). Then he said he wanted to move to Tel Aviv. I asked him how he thought he would manage until he could make it as an actor and he told me that you just need to know with whom to go to bed. So I told him that that is prostitution, and I asked him if that was what he wanted to become, a prostitute ... Yes, I am as direct a person as you are. Then he told me, "If this is what I need to do to get out of here, then that's what I'll do." And he said that he does not have any problem with getting into bed in order to succeed ... After, we went for a walk together, and I asked him when he feels he can be without masks, so he said, "When I shut myself in my room alone and listen to music." (Sound familiar?) It was like getting a glimpse of my entire childhood in an instant. Then I asked him if he had been hurt during his childhood. I did not say sexual abuse; I did not say what kind of injury. But he told me before that he wants to be seen, so I saw him ... He immediately said yes, he did not deny it for a moment, and there was tremendous relief in his voice ... Of course, he had formed a script about the injury for himself, one that did not mesh with reality ... I know, I felt in his words that he created a scenario for himself that he can live with ... But it's okay, the fact that he confirmed this injury is tremendous progress. What is interesting is that I never directly mentioned "sexual abuse," and yet, that is what he stated outright, sexual abuse ... I can see from his situation that it can end poorly. If he ends up in Tel Aviv and does what he wants to do, it will end very badly! I've been there, I know how slippery this slope is ... And he's not me. He is just like my friends; he will not survive it ... And even if he does manage to survive it, he will be filled with such trauma afterward that there might not even be much to do for him later on ... And I wonder what to do ... He chose me ... And I know that when we choose someone, they are very significant ... I am a social worker and I cannot ignore his pain, and I, Ziv, cannot ignore his pain ... You understand, it is not the therapist who chooses their patients, but rather the patient chooses who they will let treat them ... And at all levels ... He did not do anything to me ... And I feel I have to transcend myself in ways

I have never done before ... Tell me, Rachel, is this not surreal? Tell me if this is happening or has happened to someone else ... It is just unbelievable ... I do not know what to feel or think about it, I just know it's not real and I had to write it down to release it from my system, because I cannot concentrate on anything ... You see what happens in the end? Now I need to use the most narcissistic word that exists because I just do not have the ability to think of a different word ... I have to save his son! And no one can tell me not to ... And I could go ... I went through this, I cannot go and leave him to deal with this alone, not after all the time it took him to choose me in order to feel less alone. It is clear to me that his choice to confide in me was not a simple one. He does not know me at all, this is the second time in his entire life that he has even seen me ... I know, but after the meeting today, I must say, I was a little shocked at the situation ... But I'm proud of myself that I did not enter a dissociative state and I was present all throughout the conversation ... And I saw him ... It did something to me that I saw him and I did not disappear ... And at the end of the conversation, he said the sentence to me that showed that he chose me, "You're not like everyone else."

21:10
Tomorrow, I will sit down to write down everything that occurred to me at the meeting. I can tell you that there were two levels of talking going on ... But it was interesting, and there was a moment that I was just looking at the entire conversation from the outside ... But not from a dissociative place, but rather from a professional's viewpoint. It was amazing to see what was going on there ... But the most important point was that the conversation was lively and flowed without a hint of threat or aggression, and the communication that we conducted was just like it was during the abuse ... It's like riding a bike; I knew it would be a safe and familiar place and I was right. Everything was said there, everything I wanted, and he answered in his own way ... And there was a kind of clash on an unconscious level of the conversation, and then at some point it created separation ... And then everything calmed down ... And I can tell you, from the outside, I saw his dissociation ... He was and he wasn't present. I could see that his parts were mixed-up ... He remembered and didn't remember anything ... As you say, "You are telling without telling." Then he

remembered and did not really remember ... He has a movie in his head ... It's incredible.

22:00
Exactly as he said, my cousin was with them all the time and he would take him to the beach and to eat ... Then my aunt looked at him shocked and said, "What are you talking about? It was not him, it was Zahavit who was here all the time." I must say that it was fascinating ... On a professional level, it was fascinating ... You must be asking yourself how in such a situation could I even be thinking in this way ... So I'll tell you, my parts were connected and my senses were so sharp that it even fazed me at first, but I was really focused on my goal, and after that, I felt safe in my place. The curious part of me came out and I had to dissect what was happening in that room. And I felt some anxiety, but my conduct was so relaxed and everything was so quiet, and then, they too relaxed in my presence ... You know, you can speak simply and say all that needs to be said in a quiet way, one that is non-threatening and indirect ... Maybe it was said quietly, but words spoken quietly can be shouted as well ... This is the abuse ... Silence that makes a lot of noise. And when I left, I gave him a hug that was clearly very distant and gentle ... It was not the girl's hug or full of love or longing; it was a hug with a goal ... And it was a brief touch for about a second, it was not quite a hug but more like an approach of sorts ... It was not comfortable and it was not pleasant. But something in me said that I needed to do it ... I don't know if it was unnecessary or not ... I really have no idea. But it did not add or detract. It could be that I have yet to understand the purpose it served, for better or worse ... Meanwhile, it is neither-nor ... What is important is that my brain adapted to the image that I have of him today, and it no longer has the image I had in my head. Now it has the image of someone else; someone very tired and worn out and old ... I no longer see him as he once was ... And I can no longer see him that way ... What mattered was that he would not be frozen into a dissociation as he was, and that I managed to obtain that ... I was proud of myself about how I conducted myself :)

23:00
I will write in parts -- with your permission.

When I got there, I climbed the stairs. I preferred to take the stairs rather than the elevator; it was symbolic that this was my choice. I had the feeling that with each step I was collecting the parts in me, my thoughts, and emotions. There was something gathering as I ascended the stairs... gathering and unifying. And when I stood in front of the locked door, I felt I should knock on the door quickly and not wait, like ripping off a Band-Aid quickly, so it hurts less. So this was the same thing; I stood in front of the door less than ten seconds, I took a deep breath, I don't think I had ever breathed like that in my life, and I just put out my hand. The first thing that greeted me with my first step was the smell, a really strong smell, just as I remembered it. This caused me to have mixed feelings. On the one hand, it is a familiar smell, but on the other hand, it is a familiar scent that I do not wish to remember. And it took me a minute to reset my sense of smell and to calm myself; it was very intense. Then he stood in front of me and I looked at him and I did not recognize him. He did not look at all like the figure that I had in my mind, like the image that he was ... I saw a very old and worn-out man with very tired eyes ... I was in shock. I felt awed at how my brain was trying to piece the puzzle together; it was not easy ... It had been many years since we last saw each other ... And the once or twice that we had seen each other up until this meeting, I dissociated, and therefore, I saw him as he was in my head; my brain could not make a link to what was actually being seen. But this time I did not disconnect, and it felt like my brain was receiving a lot of information in a very short amount of time, I mean really short. I disconnected, but it was very slight. I was present the entire time and this is what I wanted. The disconnect was only in order to match up the past and the present. And when there was anxiety in the room and he just left it there, I could not ask for more control and coping mechanisms than I had ... During this part, I feel that the mechanism did not disappoint me, but I, too, did not let myself down. I can say that my cognitive portion was very dominant and my emotional one was working more on the sensory level ... Because, at first, I wanted at least to be able to see what was in front of me and what I was dealing with, I studied the area in very fine detail and felt that I had the flexibility to deal with the situation. It's so different to come from a place of strength than from a place of fear; it is amazing. Even more amazing was that the conversation took place on several levels. I saw clearly my uncle in a dissociative state. There were moments where he was my beloved uncle, and others where he was not present at all, and below the surface, he was the uncle I knew ... He was in constant flux between the three states, and I watched how his identity see-sawed, I felt instability in his conduct ... I think it surprised him ... My actions surprised him. On the one hand, I engaged in a normal conversation with him, while on the other hand, under the surface, I was engaging in an altogether different conversation ... I do not think that he expected it; it surprised him and caused him to lose the ability to control various parts of himself ... Since he is on the level of black and white ... He was thinking that I remember and I'll attack him, or that I do not remember then everything is fine with him ... But the way the conversation was being held did not allow for any part of him to be dominant. He was caught in the middle. And at some very critical junctures in the conversation, my aunt, underneath the surface, formed a coalition with me. Although I do not think it was ever a conscious decision ... But it did affect him. Every time he said something from his memory that exists in the film running through his head, my aunt corrected him, and it always had something to do with me; I saw the startled look on his face. I think if I was coming from an emotional and aggressive place, I could not have seen what was happening in any sort of way. He had a surprised look in his eyes as if he was hearing these things for the very first time ... I saw the movement he was making between reality and what was going on in his head. And I also was engaged in a movement of sorts, in the covert conversation that was taking place there, but I refused to give up, and although I engaged in a delicate balancing act of what to say and how to say it, I said everything that I wanted to say. And I looked him in the eyes when I said it. I felt how the power was with me this time, on so many levels, mental, emotional and cognitive, and even in my connection to myself. Without a doubt, the power was definitely in my hands. And I used it in several dimensions. One was to protect me and to stay focused on my purpose for being there, because that was what was important. The second was to make him say all the things that I wanted him to say without him feeling threatened. Basically, he confirmed so many things in his gaffes here that I do not think there would have been any other way for him to reveal them. And I do not think he ever consciously knows about their existence at that level that he would talk about them. When he didn't say something, my aunt would fill in the blank. And third, I sat up straight with confidence, without fear, staring directly at him without lowering my gaze or averting my eyes ... In my opinion, there were several levels for me to win over him. One of them was to look directly into his eyes; he was the one that lowered them, either consciously or unconsciously. Not that it matters. What mattered is that I remained steadfast in front of him. This meeting was almost a complete role reversal. And I know that there are many emotions that accompany this meeting, and I know I feel them on both conscious and unconscious levels ... But during all the abuse and during my entire life in general, I have been running on emotional peaks, for better or for worse. But this time, I feel a different type of control. I'm not falling out of balance, I am giving a place to all of the emotions, and I dance with each one, moving from one to the other in a gentle manner ... This had never happened to me before today, something changed in me, something relaxed ... And I will share the situation and I'll explain how I saw it and I how I see it now ... I started a conversation about sexual assault, but, from an external perspective, it had nothing to do with me or anyone who was sitting in the house. And I wanted to test their responses, so I could make adjustments to what would be discussed further ... And the responses were varied. My aunt brushed off the assault with humor, and, basically, she told me that she is with me up to a point, but there are things that she just cannot take in ... In her own way, she told me that she was disconnected and she was not able to listen or to be present. His son reacted angrily and blamed the victims, and, from his response, I understood that he is not in a good place internally and he could not digest this information. My uncle was ambivalent; he fluctuated between blaming the attacker and blaming the victim. He really was not focused enough to comment about it. And then, at some point, his son told him to keep quiet before he ended up in the newspaper or on TV ... My uncle looked at me and said, "Who would complain about me today, at my age?" From this, I heard and saw his concealed anxiety, and he was trying to send me the message of "have mercy on me". And this was the point of the role reversal. This is what I wanted, that he would ask for my mercy ... I wrote to you that this is what I want, and this is what happened at that very moment ... Then I answered him with a double-edged meaning, I told him and myself that not long ago, and when I say "not long ago," I mean before I got there ... I felt anger and rage at such people. Today, at this moment, I pity those people who need to hurt children and women in order to feel strong. I answered him on two levels: the first being, if you want mercy then you shall receive mercy, something that you have not given me, I am now giving you, I'm better than you. I feel sorry for you, now you have become smaller than me. And the second meaning is that I'm not going to report you; that's not my goal. And from that moment, I knew I controlled the conversation, and I orchestrated it like a conductor, signaling all the instruments ... My violin connected at that moment, and in real-time, I adjusted the strings ... Finally, I managed to make the music that I wanted to hear ... The painting of the violin finally clicked ... Just like the feather tipped the scales to one side, this time the scales were tipped in my favor ... I placed the feather ... And it was a feather, because it was so delicate, not heavy and violent ... It was nice for me, for my feelings and thoughts ... I used my most powerful tool, the mind, cognition ... And more than that, I suddenly realized that in this interaction I became him. His part came out and did to him exactly what he did to me for years. Just as he was the lover and the attacker, I basically answered him on two levels, one was relaxing and the other one took away his control. What it took him years to do, I accomplished in just one conversation. I turned it into my means, my tool ... For a moment, I let him feel what I felt for years ... It was amazing, because something else happened there as well ... I took his part out and left it there when I exited the house. The part that was less positive. The part that was more positive I kept, because it is a part of me, but I left there the not-so-good part ... I threw it back, because it is not part of me and it's not part of who I want to be when I grow up. This was an entirely different experience. I cannot describe in words; I do not know how to give it words ... But when I write, things suddenly make sense in my head ... And other parts surface as well ... It was a complex meeting, and I need more time to process it all ... And in between worrying, as you said (I listen closely to your every word) about the difficulty involved in change ... I'm really trying to be balanced and to be attentive to myself in order to increase my sense of calm and reduce the anxiety involved in the fear of change ... Until today, I have made quite a lot of changes, in actuality, each change has been an introduction to this change ... And still, it is a significant change, so I'm very attentive to all the parts, even to those which change is very difficult for them ... Meanwhile, everything is calm ... But there is a certain amount of tension in me, guarding this achievement. I worked very hard for it ...

23:30
I feel like I am repeating myself, but I am speechless. I really agree with the description, and I am surprised at how quickly you are aware of so many dimensions. And you left him to himself and you used his strength against him. This is the meaning of the word "reframing," there is no deletion of introverted parts, but rather you utilize them in favor of the right objectives and control.

23:40
I do not lose anything that comes to mind or enters my emotions ... So every time the conversation below the surface peaked ... I felt his flooding; he really could not contain the interaction. On the one hand, it was familiar, but on the other hand, it was completely new. He got up and went to get something to eat or drink, or alternatively, my aunt sent him ... It's very interesting, because, at first, I said no, I do not need anything ... But then I took a deep breath and tried to see what was going on there, and I realized that it was to reduce anxiety. This is a pattern in the house used to reduce anxiety. I very quickly understood the link between conduct during childhood that every time after the abuse, he would bring me food, symbolically, it was to shut me up ... This is a creation of silence without saying it explicitly. I did not think it was right to break this pattern, because it helped the situation flow well. Actually, I left him and my aunt all the familiar places. What broke was the cycle inside of me, and the change projected outwards; I ate and drank, but I did not keep quiet. I simply watched the scene; I watched some moments from the inside and other moments from the outside ... It was amazing, just like the process that I went through and am going through, I look inside, go outside to do processing, and then I return ... So that every entry

and exit is connected together, yet each part is differentiated from the one that follows. I feel the interaction there created fragments that I recognized because of the behavior ... His uncontrollable urge to get up every time I said something that had a double meaning, something beneath the surface; it caused chaos among his parts. It showed me his weaknesses ... Just as he did it to me ... And I was right; he is as much of a captive as I was ... Only when I arrived there, I had one leg out of the cage ... Now, I also know why there is no key in any of the pictures ... Because the key is with me. Not with him. I have it. I kept it all these years just in preparation for this moment; I put him back into the cage and took the key with me.

Indeed, he left the cage long ago, but he had his cage, regardless of our joint cage. At this meeting, I brought him back to his cage, I locked it and I took the key. It's true that I still have my cage. I am not ignoring it for a moment and this also requires hard work ... But it was without his cage ... I will manage with mine ... I will work on it and I will find my way out of it. Do you remember that I wrote you something about him that was hurtful and I told you that no one could see it? And it's for your eyes only? The fact that he is in captivity means that, actually, he belongs to my group, whether I like it or not. I think that my writing released something in me ... I felt that I am writing everything that I have in my mind and in my heart ... And it wasn't simple, the writing gives me the ability to see things differently ... I always thought this, but when I wrote to you, it gave me a kind of internal validity and I started to understand things differently. I think you gave me a place, from the beginning, to express things that I did not have the courage to say anywhere else, and it helped me a lot ... You always say that a therapist should be prepared to hear these pornographic elements of a story. I agree with you one hundred percent, even more ... But not only does the therapist need to hear and accept things which are beyond his common sense ... And this is what you have; this is your ability. I am not sure that other therapists would have the same ability to contain it. This place gave me the confidence to face everything that came afterwards. Thank you :). And I do not know why I wrote what I wrote now, but if I connect it to what I wrote above, so it was my experience with you that gave me the ability to absorb their unconscious, silencing experience without being swallowed by it ... even to use this pattern to continue the hidden conversation ... I think I gave them, and especially him, the chance to behave in the most natural way, and I was able to manipulate the situation better. And the moment that I succeeded to get him back into the cage, it was a defining moment ... Because he had not been in this cage for quite some time, but I know every part of it, every point and speck of dust inside the cage. I brought him to my space. And it's amazing. Think about it, I was in a physical place that was not neutral ... It was his home, their home ... I managed to disconnect physically, and I took him emotionally and mentally to my home. The house that he created ... The closed house. I put him back in it. But this time, my tree top was looked from above the house at moments and it looked from within the house at times. I think his return entry into the cage created a form of emotional chaos for him ... And I worried about entering the cage with him as he showed me the house and walked with me from room to room ... I acted as he did, but I did it below the surface. He did it physically and I gave it back to him secretly.

29.5.12

6:30

I do not know if I'm right or not ... But this is my gut feeling ... Do you think that Miri, my therapist, feels that I took my termination from her? On the one hand, it's my life and I decide what my path is and what is right for me ... And I chose well and correctly, and I feel totally complete with the path that I chose. On the other hand, she worked with me for six years and, at the end, she was only a party in the final part ... I think that part of the confidence that I had in order to finish this process is because of her. But maybe I hurt her? I did not have therapy with her for a week and a half, so I could not really ask her ... I do not know what to ask, or even if it is alright to ask ... Maybe she is happy for me that I managed to finish the process? Maybe it's a bit too late, but it is important to me to know how she feels. She is important to me and I feel that maybe it was a surprise to her and she did not have time to adapt to it ... You see, I told her about my meeting with my uncle, the abuser, and then she spoke to me on the telephone and she could not meet with me before the meeting, and when we met, it was afterward ... I do not know if she also had to adapt to this ... Perhaps the process is reciprocal, and it is not just mine? Maybe, and this sounds weird, maybe in a particular way, because she was with me during captivity, she had to go through some kind of a gradual process to depart from it? Maybe it affects her, even if she didn't mention it? It's not that I am concerned about her, she receives supervision ... It's just sitting in my stomach, so I wrote about it to you ... When we spoke on the telephone before the meeting, she was not sure that I would succeed and she was concerned about me ... Maybe she also projected her feelings onto me without any connection to me? I really do not know ...

6:45
So maybe the right thing to do is to have a conversation between the two of you and to bring up all of your emotions, feelings, understandings and insights? Something interesting is happening in terms of your role to her which is a result of change and integration of all your parts.

6:55
Regarding Miri ... I'll tell you what I feel, and it could be that I am making a big mistake, but these are my gut feelings ... For six years, she worked with me in intensive therapy which, probably, drew her into the trauma. And I just got up and left the trauma without going through with her some kind of "orderly" departure process with her. I really did not think it would happen so quickly ... I did not really aim for that, it just happened that way. And I do not regret it for a moment. But when I look back for a moment, maybe I hurt her, without intending to do so. I just wanted to get out of captivity; I could not be there any longer. But if she was with me during captivity, then I basically abandoned her at the end of the process ... In my experience, she went through the process of breaking free of my mother's captivity with me, which was a different process completely. I do not know how to explain it, but I could not think about the figure that I had for a mother for a long time, and she helped me get out of this captivity. I understood that I released myself

from her captivity, and I did not think that I would need to go back inside again in order for her to help me to leave his captivity ... My feelings are that I did to her what my uncle did to me, in a way. I left her in captivity and left it, one could say, without prior notice. When it happened, I just felt a moment of courage; I was either to survive or to stop existing and I had to jump into the departure process. But I left her behind ... Since I met with him, I have a strange feeling that she is distancing herself from me ... Maybe she trying to send me a message that she is angry with me, maybe it's just in my head ... I really do not know ... But even if she is angry, I understand her ... I meet with her every Monday, and this Monday we did not arrange a meeting. I sent her a message and she said she was on vacation with her children, and she will get back to me with another time to meet. She knows that I work and she wanted to arrange a meeting in the middle of the day ... And then it was postponed until Friday. I do not think she's aware of what is happening. I do not think that she thinks that I feel this way. I love her very much. I do not feel guilty about the process or about what I did ... From my understanding, she is supposed to be the therapist and an adult; she has to deal with it ... No therapy has clear rules; there are also surprises along the way ... And I think that she should be well prepared for surprises ... And somehow, this feeling accompanies me that maybe she experienced, to some degree (it is clear to me that I don't know exactly), what I experienced when the abuse ended ... I really think that the process of leaving captivity is a reciprocal one with a therapist ... I think that the therapist needs it as much as his patient does ... Maybe she felt the loss of Ziv as she was. But today, I am a different Ziv ... I do not know ... maybe it's just my feeling and only in my head ...

8:45
I understand what you're saying. It seems that you need to meet her and tell her everything that you are feeling. You are not doing to her what he did to you. The change happened in parallel, and it could be hard. Nevertheless, the change is positive. You matured and you are free; spread your wings. This is the goal of therapy. And when the client achieves the purpose for which he came, joy and the sense of relief fill the dialogue, both for the therapist and the client. So do not worry, when you meet,

speak, and if nothing comes out, write it down.

1.6.12

12:30
How are you? Did you meet with Miri?

12:32
I will meet with her in two hours … I had an anxiety attack during the night. Now, I am alright.

12:33
Is the anxiety connected to Miri?

12:34
Yes, I think so, but I am not sure. It was a short attack and it passed … But yes, I am a little nervous about the meeting.

15:00
So I was in therapy. The anxiety really came from there. I told Miri that I wrote to you about what happened in therapy and she gave me permission, so I should feel free to share. I asked her how she felt about all that has happened in the recent months, if she is angry with me or feels that I hurt her. At first she did not understand what I meant, and then I explained to her how I feel and what I have been feeling over the last two weeks. She told me that she was not angry and she was very proud of me. So I told her that I know she loves me and is proud of me, but I asked her how she feels, not what she feels about me. So she divided it into three parts, and she said that, in terms of her mind, she is really happy for me and she thinks that I went through an amazing process. In terms of emotions, she had concerns and when I started the process with you, she understood that I have another mother, besides her, and this was not easy for her. And she feared it would harm our process (mine and hers). Apparently, it made her feel uncertain. And then there is the middle which combines her emotions and her mind, and in the middle, she said that I succeeded in creating a separation between my relationship with her and my relationship with you, and, in the end, she does not feel a change in our relationship. Then, I asked her if she still

has something she wants to tell me, because she has been my therapist for so many years already and then relatively quickly I started a process with you. She told me that I did not do it out of the blue. Since I met you, I have been preparing her for this, that I have found another safe place other than with her. And she went back to what I said about you and my place with you. It was new, I did not remember it. And she said I prepared her for this when I was leaving this therapy to try out another therapy. This facilitated her acceptance of the change in therapy. She told me that I was a child and became a teenager. I told her my feelings that, basically, because we have spent so much time together, I felt that, in some sense, it would be hard for her to release me. And this is my experience that I received from my mother, and I had to obtain independence through my own strengths. I told her that my healing experience with her was related to mother and that my healing experience with you was related to him. And I asked her if it surprises her, because every therapy session was about the abuse. She didn't answer this question, and I didn't feel the need to push. I explained to her that talking with her and writing to her about the abuse was, for me, related to the healing process about my mother, and less focused on the actual abuse itself. I explained that I needed to be the girl who included her mother in what she went through in order to correct the silence and the secret … And when she responded to me as a mother is supposed to respond to her child who tells her a secret like that, I felt that I could be released from the feelings of guilt that accompanied me because of the secret. And when I spoke to her and I wrote to her it affected my understanding of the abuse, but consciously or more correctly, subconsciously, I wanted to tell my mother and I wanted my mother to hug me. And her response was exactly what I needed, but in order to leave his captivity, I had to go out, because she is a mother who cares and protects, and I didn't think that she could release me in order to meet with him. She did not deny that last sentence; she even said that as a mother it was hard for her to let me go see him, that she might not have initiated such a meeting. But when it came from my side, and after our conversation, she realized that I was ready and she needed to trust me. And she told me that she always trusts me. But my meeting with him was a surprise for her and she was not ready for it. Although she is very supportive of me, it still surprised her. And her maternal instinct was to protect me from it. I told her that exactly for this reason I decided to leave my safe place, because I felt ready and I knew that my mother would not release me so easily. Especially not to a place that is threatening. I explained to her that I needed another mother who will push me to go out of my shell. I explained to her that I chose you because, from the beginning, I felt things would be different with you, and I was right. Then, I told her I do not watch pornography anymore and that my food preferences have changed completely. I did not want to tell her at first, because I wanted to know that it is true and that it would last, and now I feel more confident to share it, because I did not want to disappoint anyone ... In the end, she told me that she loves me and she was in tears ... She said that I successfully worked on myself in two therapeutic spaces without hurting anyone in either space. She told me not to worry, because all along the way I was worried about her, and she was ready for me to go through a process with you. She said that I was sensitive enough all along the way to ask her how she felt and to let her know where I was during my process, and in this way, I was able to mentally prepare her properly.

17:00
Hi

Thanks for sharing.

I'm glad that we can evaluate the conversation. I am debating whether it is my right to respond to what you wrote, because I do not think it's a good idea for me to meddle in the connection between you two. I can think or analyze by myself throughout the process about what is happening and its meaning, but I do not think it is right or fair. Therefore, I really wanted to meet with Miri within the last month or so, just as I have told you, because you are in simultaneous therapy sessions and I have to check with her to see how she feels about it.

A lot of changes have occurred in your relationships with other people in the world as a result of the changes you're going through and that you will go through. It is somewhat like recovery from a long hard illness. Slowly, one discovers that there is more power, more energy, new insights and a different perception of relationships and of oneself. This process is not easy, and sometimes it is frightening and causes anxiety like a flood during the night. It involves the loss of what is familiar and causes one's entry into empty and different situations and different relationships with others. Maybe it's like growing pains. The plus side is that, for the most part, it will pass with time. On the downside, there is no way back even if one wants to go back. Just like what you wrote about the degree, where is the disconnection when you need it? My favorite book as a child was <u>Pollyanna</u>, and she said that every bad thing has some good to it and all good things need a little bad in order to understand and appreciate the good. Personally, I believe this is how things are.

17:30
Rachel, you can respond if you like. I told Miri that I think it would be good if everything that happens between us (her and me) will also appear in the book. She agreed with me. I know that there are many good things in my relationship with her, I love her and I am very attached to her and apparently there are few things as good as that. I think that it stems from the strong connection that we have, and that this is okay, any long-term and intimate relationship has good things and a few not so good things (assuming that the relationship is healthy). She is a great therapist, and I think that because of her concern, I had the courage to work outside of our relationship. When I think about it, she gave me the sense of security that she would be there for me throughout the process. This was really a kind of growth, the ability to leave and the feeling that I always have somewhere to return to. I told her that part of my corrective experience with mother was exactly this place, the place where I could leave and then come back … You understand that this was never the case with my mother, I did not experience youth … I was my mother's mother, and I took care of her day and night, so I did not have the opportunity to experience a normal adolescence, one of independence and one of leaving our mother-daughter relationship. I was stuck. And it was precisely the therapy room where I felt the safest and most protected and the sense of security that I could leave, try things out, and return with a different perspective. And the experience was corrective, as Miri was accepting of not only my departure but also the change. Actually, maybe it was not corrective, but it was an initial experience. You see, when my mother died I went through a rebellious period, but then I did not have the sense of security nor a place to return … And now, it was something else. I think that she is okay with the

whole process, and I am really happy that she shared with me how she felt. I also asked her to share with me without worrying about what to say; I told her that I can contain it and it's important for me to know. And I think that she fulfilled her part. She shared with me and told it to me in the parts as I prefer. :) She did not try to cover up her feelings. I felt that she shared everything; I felt that we had a real conversation and it was amazing for me. It is clear to me that on one hand she said less pleasant things to me, and on the other hand, it was what I expected to hear from a mother. Even so, for me, there is a gap between how things should be done from a professional standpoint and what I want from the person who will help me have a corrective experience about my relationship with my mother. You see, it's clear to me that it is not so good when she says to me that as a mother it was hard for her to let me go to the place of pain. On the other hand, her concern is precisely what made me feel that, in that place, someone cares for me. After talking to her, I feel that I did the right thing; the whole process was just as it should have been. In fact, the departure and my coming to you was the smart and informed choice, I am happy that I made it. I managed to create an intimate space with you, and it was easier to create this space with you, also because of and thanks to Miri. You see, I created an intimate place with her after a lot of work, and, in the end, when I really started to tell her about the trauma, it was accompanied by a huge amount of anxiety, because it was the first time I told mother what happened there. I had many mixed feelings about sharing my experiences. On the one hand, I wanted to tell, and on the other hand, I constantly was afraid of the reaction to the experiences I was narrating ... And then, when she responded to it in such a containing and empathetic way, I was able to leave and come to you and feel more secure in the intimate relationship that I created with you in such a short period of time. I didn't have to go through the whole path with you. When I came to you, I was ready. I do not know if I am explaining myself in an understandable way. My relationship with Miri was very complex, but within the relationship I had everything I needed to go out and create intimacy with other people. And with you, I realized how much it can flow and how it can be deep and intimate. In the end, it's all related to choices,

I needed to choose the right person, and I chose. I told Miri that I love you very much and I am bound to you, but from another place than I am connected to her, and I feel a more mature relationship with you and this is new for me ... I have never been on the receiving end, even as an adult, and I have devoted myself to accept this. This is new and refreshing, and even very nice. I do not trust adults much, but I managed to produce something else with you. You should know that it really moves me. Look, I went through all my serious anxieties, fears and corrections that were related to my mother with Miri, and I am still going through it, as you see.

When I came to you, I could already see another mother in you ... Because I did not have the fears and anxieties connected to mother anymore ... The construction of our intimate connection was created in a faster and smoother way ... The process was faster; I think that the process was amazing. It still resonates within me ... It was like pulling a bandage from a wound, it was quick and less painful, it didn't become stretched or stretch me ... There was something comforting; I was able to dive in with you and not drown, but be able to find the way up ... And I think that like in any relationship, Miri and I are very confident in our relationship. I also never gave her the feeling that she needs to worry about the relationship ... I tried to make a separation.

20:50
I think that Miri was a major part of the healing experience. There are things that I think the context of wanting to tell Mother and not wanting to tell her, and the need to protect Mother and protect her from yourself that came up in the text that you wrote which is not a criticism, but it is part of your role, which was and is and always will be. Protecting those who take on the role of helper, whether it is you or someone else, will continue in therapy. While protecting your mother, the need also to protect others from harm and your constant concern of whether you hurt someone will not arise from the need for forgiveness; it comes from your directness and readiness to raise the issues and bring them to the table, which always will help you to deal with the anxiety. Do you remember that you told me, in the beginning, that your uncle was your mother's favorite person? This is in itself a very clear message not to tell, but in fact we never really spoke about

the clues or messages that you sent to your mother and she did not see or understand them, or she responded in a way that prevented a direct discussion. There are other points, such as from where and from whom did you, nevertheless, learn to put things on the table and talk about them? I think that you actually learned it from your uncle, in an upside–down way. He laid out his desires and his views very bluntly and directly, and you learned to use this ability positively. This is a professional concept, called reframing.

22:50
Yes, there is a part of me that cannot hurt anyone. When I hurt it is accompanied by difficult feelings for me. Maybe I always find myself being careful not to hurt others and always asking for forgiveness ... I just behave in the opposite manner to the way they treated me. Do you know how people have to ask for my forgiveness for what they did to me? But there is a moment when there no longer is the need or desire to get it from them. There is a moment when it does not matter anymore ... I'm worried that this moment will not come ... You know, my mother always was ill and I did everything for her; I tried to say the right things, to listen to her and I know that she loved me, but she was not a mother to me. And for years, I experienced a feeling that maybe I did not do enough, and that, basically, what happened to me in childhood was my punishment. She became ill and died because of me ... And when she was sick, there was a part that hurt her, and I used it to do it ... There is a part that loves her and there is a part that does not know and does not remember what I am supposed to love ... When she was sick, what happened with my uncle remained between us. My pain was sidelined, she became the focus. I was afraid that if she discovered it, her illness would only get worse and she would die because of me ... So I absorbed it all in silence, without uttering a word ... when she died, I was very angry with her, because I did everything for her to live and then she gave up ... I felt that she gave up on me ... She was supposed to remain with me for a little bit longer ... She went too fast ... I felt abandonment and failure ... That's why I hid inside myself. I could not stand anyone or their presence next to me ... Do you know what it is like to be with a sick person for 24 hours, to delete everything that comes your

way, your feelings in order to treat them? And at the same time to experience abuse? And I also had to keep a secret with her. A different secret, but still, I was keeping a secret ... I had to keep secret how she really was feeling and how she really was behaving ... When there was no one around but me and her ... I had to lie to everyone and say everything's fine when everything was not fine ... Between him and her I just wanted to die, every night I would pray that I would not wake up in the morning ... And then I would feel guilty that I even was thinking that, because if I died, who would care for her? It reached a point where, in fact, being with him freed me from her captivity ... That with him I could feel what I could not do with her ... And then seeing everyone come as if nothing was happening, each in his own life, coming to visit and life is good for them and flowing for them ... And I am the only one stuck between two systems of captivity ... Then my mom says to me in my ear, "I'd love it if they would just leave. It's hard for me that they are here; I want to be myself again." I also wanted to be me again ... But I didn't have myself to go back to ... And you know what "myself" she wanted to go back to? The depressive self who didn't stop talking about death ... Who was angry at the world ... And do you know who everyone in the world is? Me, I am the world because it's me that absorbed it ... She would scream from pain during the nights and if there was a night that I didn't wake up to help her, she would not talk to me all day ... You understand, I didn't sleep at all during the nights and then there was one night when I collapsed ... I had to learn to handle it from night to night ... And there was my uncle ... And there was the house ... And there was the rest of the family ... And then maybe there was also myself ... I did not have much left but I took what there was ... She was lucky that I already was skilled in keeping secrets ... And maybe she already knew, who knows ... Before she got sick, I remember that I was sick a lot, nearly all of the time, and especially after he was with me ... I think that's how I tried to show her that something was wrong ... Because when one is sick, then something is wrong ... But it didn't do anything for her; it was even comfortable for her ... Because I stayed beside her ... And she liked that I was beside her, because she was controlling and possessive of me. I shut myself in the room all day; I almost never left the house ... She did not see this either. To her, I was a little girl who was a little inhibited who loved to be at home. When he came to take me, there were situations where I resisted going with him, then she would convince me to go ... Because it is not nice to behave that way ... She would always tell me that I was a fat girl and I had to lose weight ... Rachel, I was not fat, not even chubby ... But she wanted me to go on a walk with her every day and that I would eat according to a diet ... She would humiliate me in front of my brothers and they learned from her, so they came down on me ... I did not remember it, only now, as I write this to you, I am reminded of it ... When she got sick, it stopped because my brothers were hardly there ... And she, she was only preoccupied with herself ... I would say that at least she saw me ... It's better to be transparent ... My uncle always was admiring the way I looked ... He was the antidote to what she did ... Strange, isn't it? It was impossible to speak with her; she was closed off to emotions, or at least my emotions ... I'm not saying that there were no nice moments with her ... But you know, the bad ones left their mark. In general, I always tried to talk to her, but it became a conversation about her and her pain ... She never listened to my pain ... Even before her illness ... Her pain came first ... I think that no matter how I showed her what I was going through she was just not in the space to see anything ... I think that, at some point, I stopped trying to show her, because I understood that she would not see it ... How disappointing ... You know, even as a child, there was a moment where I no longer had expectations, I was simply accepting what happened ... And I admit that I accepted it; I didn't try to fight or resist it ... I was not trying to show anything ... There was a moment when I lost hope that something would change ... The only thing that kept me going was music, because it helped me dive into myself so deeply that even I could not manage to see my outer self ... And it was comfortable for all those involved ... And with Miri it was different ... Because she hugged me and comforted me and listened to me ... Miri is not similar to my mother at all and it's a good thing ...

From whom did I learn to put things out there ... Certainly not from anyone in my family ... Probably a lot of my confidence came from my uncle ... He was full of confidence, and he passed it onto me in his own way ... And my time on the street added to this ability ... But I can tell you that, in fact, when I was alone with myself in the room, I learned to confront myself ... And I think that, at some stage, it just radiated outwards ... When I was alone, I had no masks, no lies ... And I looked the truth straight in the eyes ... I could not do anything, but I never ignored its presence ... And I think that the therapy with Miri really helped me to develop this place ... Because I felt secure enough to be me ... And I think that my mother and he had a significant influence on my conduct ... Both were very domineering and possessive of me ... And I learned from them what is power and strength ... I cannot behave as they behaved towards me ... So I'm doing the opposite to what they did ... Since my childhood, I am alone ... As I got older, I realized that part of coping is to put everything out there, which is basically the best way to cope ... I believe that there were a lot of factors that allow me to be very open and direct today ... But the ability is mine only ... And my courage is mine only ... Just because something gave you tools does not mean that you will use them ... or that you will used them correctly ... what I did with them is my business ...

23:00
Due to the fact that I took care of her, I can understand that she is grateful ... but that I kept a secret? You see, I could not accept it that she thanked me or was proud of me for it ... How can I be? Even if she was, I have no desire for this gratitude ... Rachel, it is getting thanks for the fact that she preferred someone else over her daughter ... Who prefers someone over his own child? If that's how she's proud of me, I'd rather not have it ... I did it because it had to be done, and a lot of it was for her ... But if she preferred him to me, and this is what she thanked me for, then I'll save myself the insult ... When you or Miri tell me that you are proud of me, it is much more significant for me than what I got from her ... So pay attention for a moment to what you wrote to me ... That she was proud of me because I took care of her and because I kept her secret ... She was proud of me only because it was about her and for her ... Not because it was something that I did for her ... Even her gratitude and pride were, in a sense, anti-social ... I did it for her, so she is proud of me? And what about what I did for myself? So she said to me that my sister was better and my brother

was better ... And that is okay, but I could do more ... So how am I supposed to look at this place? Do not think that I'm feeling confused. I am really not. I know exactly how I feel ... I feel like I did not have a mother who was dedicated to me. I do feel like I was a daughter to her. I'm not angry; I am just saying what I feel and see ... You know, when I tell someone I am proud of him, it is not because he did something for me, but it's because he did something for himself ... I know that I have to remember good things, and I remember, but not before the age of six ... There were funny moments with her ... There could not have only been bad stuff. You know, it's like with my uncle, there also were good moments ... You need to understand that I was only with her or only with him; it's impossible that it was all bad ... As you said, there is bad in everything good and there is good in everything bad ... It is pretty amazing that you wrote this, because I live in this place ... Do you know what the symbol for Yin and Yang looks like? It is one of the most beautiful symbols in the world ...

One day, maybe I was 13 years old, my mom had just had surgery and chemotherapy, and I had to take her to the bathroom and I tried, but she was heavy ... Usually, she would lean against me, but this time she could not stand ... And we both fell on the carpet and lay there and we burst out laughing ... Because to cry, I could not cry ... Especially, not next to her ... And I remember the sun warmed us as we lay there. We stayed that way for at least an hour, because she could not get up or move; it really hurt her ... And then she could not resist, and she started to cry ... I wiped her tears ... I cleaned her up and moved her to a blanket on the carpet ... And cleaned the carpet, and then I went back to lie down next to her. She patted my hand so gently ... As only a mother knows ... I know it sounds shocking, but it is one of the most beautiful moments I had with her ... And it is a moment I cannot talk about ... You can understand why, right?

2.6.12

5:00
I'll start from the end. I really understand why the memory you mentioned touches and arouses such subtle emotions. There she actually responded with gratitude and love. Most parents love their children

despite the fact that they sometimes harm their children. Notice that the word gratitude (in Hebrew) contains the word prisoner (in Hebrew). I was not trying to protect you, Ziv, and not to save you from harm, I meant every word I said. The price of exposing her secret was, in my opinion, terrible for her. Her beloved brother who abused her young daughter means choosing between loved ones, it means damaging her self-esteem and parenting skills, that is a fatal blow to her perception of what is permissible and what is forbidden, what subject one is allowed to talk about and which ones are taboo, who is a bitch and who is not, her image of her nuclear family and the family she came from, there are many prices to pay - personal, familial, social and even economic. Just so you know, most children do not share with their parents, even if it is a normal relationship, because of the shame and embarrassment and the price that parent would have to pay; and the child is afraid that the parent cannot stand it and, eventually, the child will pay the price of the parents' break down. In this respect, you saved her from knowing and needing to cope with or ignore this knowledge. For this, you deserve a big thank you. And it has nothing to do with my thoughts that parents should convey the message to their child that he can share anything with them and that they will be at his side in every situation and will protect him. A child who did not share apparently felt that the parent was unable to absorb the information or felt hurt and helpless that the parent did not see what was going on and ignored signs that he should have seen. And the child always wishes to be asked, as you ask me. And a last point that is sad but true, usually, the child who receives the least from his parents will be the child who gives most to his parents. Sarcastically, I can say that if a parent wants his child to take care of him in the future, he should give him nothing less than a loving relationship, etc. These are the children who are willing to endanger their lives for their parents and for the world at large, generally. But there is also a positive point, at least in my perception, that these are the children who also are more sensitive to the world and to others and are the best equipped to be therapists. Hug.

5:15
:) Yes ... when you are right you are right ... yes, I knew that she would not withstand it ... Today, I also understand why ... Understanding why makes it easier to understand my feelings towards her ...

11:30
This is how I see my mother ... In reality, I don't really see that she is behind the door ... You understand, in my experience, she was not even facing the handle ... She only puts her hand on the door, because she is unable to open it ... And if it was open, she would not have the legs to really go inside; even if she could open the door, she would be unable to move ... maybe it's better that she remains behind the closed door ...

11:34
Look at the picture. Do you see the hand holding a little figure behind the wall? What is the significance of the raised hand of the figure that represents your mother?

3.6.2013

8:00
What do you see in these two pictures? Are they connected?

8:20
The picture that I sent you connects me to this picture ... maybe because the different parts are very symbolic ... but for me, it reflects the picture I sent you now ... I am buried in the ground ... Mother Earth, she catches me by my legs and prevents me from

moving away from the danger ... This is truly the feeling of being stuck between a rock and a hard place ... He rules the heavens and she reigns on earth and I'm hanging in the middle ... The majority of the anger in this picture is due to the feeling of being stuck and unable to move ... I can see what is going to be but I cannot save myself ... Because the woman who was supposed to allow me to run on her land and seek refuge is the one who sacrifices me to danger ...

8:30
Can you see the outstretched hand with a small figure trapped inside? Who presents you as a victim and to whom?

8:45
I will divide the abuse into two parts: in the first part, she sacrificed me for him, in the second part; he sacrificed me for her ... The first part is the beginning of the abuse where she allowed him to abuse me ... When I was 16 and she was already in terminal condition, he returned the favor and sacrificed me for her ... What a reciprocal gesture ... They did a terrific job on me. They put me on the altar and each one, in turn, drew their sword ... But they missed my heart and mind ... Maybe that's why he stopped the abuse because she needed me more ... Apparently, they loved each other, much more than they loved me ...

On the one hand, there is a mother who loves and protects and is always there even when you need her ... She does not let me move an inch without her; and on the other hand, she is never there ... especially, when I needed her. She preferred to turn her back on me ... And it's not that she did not see, she turned her back to me. She opened the way for him, he did not have to hide or threaten or attack, the road to me was clear ... And the most painful part is that no matter what I did to please her it did not help ... because she was the one who cleared the way ... Think about how much it hurts to know that the person who you thought was the one to protect you from the world is the one who sacrifices you to be harmed ... And the pastoral colors, except for the sun, are like an arrow in the heart ... It cuts my sky ... And he, he looks at her with a kind of indifference on one hand and love on the other ... As if he expects her to direct the way ... And it's obvious that this is what she will do ... And he does not even look at me; he looks at her ... I am just an object that propels their relationship ...

12:00
I need a break from therapy ... just to give myself time to adjust to the situation I'm in now. To adapt myself to the changes that occurred in me. I want to see if I can progress without the security of therapy. Now, I want to see if I can create successfully my own self defenses ... But I'm afraid to hurt my therapist. I've never been on the other side, the side that goes ... the side that leaves. The side that ends the relationship. I have never created a real separation process ... There also is the fear of what will happen if I want to return to therapy. How can I leave and maintain a safe place for me to return to ... It's, basically, to give myself the option to return ... On the one hand it's wrong to save a place for myself in case I come back, because then maybe this knowledge will not allow me to cope and to realize my capabilities, and on the other hand, maybe I really will have to go back to continue from another starting point. The deliberations of a client: It is not easy ... it is to give up on the safest place, the most containing place that I have ever had ... At the moment, I feel that I can stand alone. I want to experience freedom from captivity without a different form of captivity. I have freedom and I want to learn and get to know this freedom. So that it will be my freedom, mine only.

Termination

Dear Rachel,

It is difficult for me to summarize the therapeutic process. It was emotional and it brought change. It was a transformational process for me. I perceive my choice of you as a therapist as my bravest decision. I knew when I met you that I could not fool you, that I would not be able to hide. Until that moment, hiding gave me safety and a sense of control. The first time we met in your office, you placed truths in front of me without trying to smooth them over, and you did not try to protect me from myself. You surprised me. I felt that this was a dialogue that allowed a soft landing. You did not treat me like a victim. You treated me like an equal who can be trusted to cope with anything. I needed a partner that could enter the hell with me, but would not stay there and would help me free myself. It was not easy for me to step out of the cage where I was entrapped by love for the perpetrator, my longing for him, and my addiction to pain and suffering, not to mention that I had to give up being alone and lonely in the world. There were moments in that process that I felt that I was losing my grasp on reality. Somehow I found myself hanging onto you and not giving up. I was afraid that you would give me up. I was afraid that you might let me go. If you had done that I would have said "she is like everyone else, all of those people who gave me up." I felt different this time. By not giving up on me, you did not enable me to give up on myself. During the whole process, you were an anchor for me. Throughout the process, you supported me, even when you corrected me when it was needed. There was something alleviating and safe in the way you treated me, not as a delicate victim of CSA or a porcelain doll, and at the same time you were sensitive to my vulnerabilities. You were very present. You treated me like an adult. I felt your respect for me. I was not worth less because I was sexually abused. You did not fear me. With you, I finally felt that whatever I might say or feel, you would not be alarmed. You were ready to hear, listen and continue. I must admit that I felt a different kind of mothering with you. You were someone who allowed me to speak my mind, and I did not fear you would abandon me.

Currently, I am aware that I am no longer guilty. I am no longer addicted to pain. I no longer automatically detach myself from difficult emotional situations. I am no longer bitter. I do not have rage attacks anymore. I feel I was released from many years of being imprisoned. I feel alive.

I want to thank you for giving me life. I want to thank you for helping me discover my creative potential. I wrote this book, because I wanted to assure that the rest of my life will be without the paralyzing pain that I used to suffer. I want to live in the present and the future, not just in the past. I want my past experience to remain in the past.

Dear Readers,

I revealed my hidden secrets. The energy invested in keeping the secret hidden prevented me from investing energy in life. I learned that it is allowed to put everything on the table, to share feelings negative and positive toward the perpetrator without fearing rejection. I decided to share my secrets with you; this shows that I have chosen life.

Dear Ziv,

It is hard for me to sum up the therapeutic process and the journey of writing the book. I have learned new principles that are required in the treatment of CSA survivors. Some of these principles contradict the current mode of treatment in terms of time, place and the role of the therapist. This experience also broadened my understanding of the uniqueness of using creative arts, specifically drawings, within the therapy. Parallel to all the professional growth, I grew as a person. I saw my boundaries as a therapist and as a person. I realized the meaning of loss for me, my limitations to contain and be in a state of helplessness, my inability to enter a state of emotional encagement, my need to preserve my cognitive and emotional independence, my ability to create intimacy and yet maintain independence, and my unconscious motives to treat CSA survivors that is connected to my personal history. I was amazed by your emotional and cognitive abilities. Your decision, which was unconscious at the beginning, to not live 30 additional years under the shadow of abuse, your persistence not to give up on yourself or on me throughout the process, your readiness to cope with your past in a new way, to confront your deepest fears, to remain loyal and authentic to yourself, showed me a new model for coping. For me, it was a challenging and satisfying experience.

I hope that the readers will feel that the content of the book will enrich them personally and professionally. I invite the readers to share their thoughts and feelings in response to the book.

Email: rlev@univ.haifa.ac.il

Part 2

Introduction

Embedded within the experience that we shared during our work, there was constant movement between rage and detachment, pain, suffering and dissociation, between past and present, feelings of power and helplessness, doing and undoing, exposure and hiding, emotion to cognitive insight, extreme emotional experience to a relaxing cognitive insight. Between roles of aggressor to victim to savior and vice versa, between a storm and calmness, distancing and closeness. The curiosity and giving in to the process became very intense as long as we proceeded. The therapy transformed into a mutual journey. The exposure of Ziv's pornographic, personal story forced me to witness and contain her life story. It forced her to return to her childhood and acknowledge that girl. Her insights throughout the process and at the end were vibrating. The uniqueness of childhood sexual abuse was seen clearly through the process in comparison to other forms of child abuse. The principles of treatment in survivors of childhood sexual abuse also became clear in terms of the therapeutic settings, such as time, intensiveness, and availability as well as in terms of the use of creative techniques and the characteristics of the verbal dialogue that need to be used, such as open questions instead of closed questions, mirroring instead of interpreting, analyzing the drawings from different angles and aspects, and understanding the interaction between symbols that were apparent in different drawings at different times. Ziv's connection between past, present, and future, and her understanding of the meaning of time within the process and stagnation versus change and growth enabled her to gain freedom. The new freedom was experienced physically (difficulties in breathing disappeared and hyper vigilance was reduced) and emotionally (depression was alleviated, anxiety disappeared, the level of dissociation was significantly reduced), behaviorally (rage attacks were reduced, sleep was calmer, addiction to pornography and specific food disappeared), and cognitively (use of first person instead of third person became more frequent when referring to herself, there were deeper understandings of the abuse and its impact). This new freedom allowed energy to be dedicated to present and future professional and personal aims. The focus of the following chapters is to describe and analyze the unique themes that characterize childhood sexual abuse, the therapeutic process, the role of the therapist, the meaning of growth and recovering, and the use of drawings as a tool for treatment of survivors of sexual abuse.

Chapter 1 - Childhood Sexual Abuse

The World Report on Violence and Health (Krug, 2002) defines sexual abuse as "any sexual act, attempt to obtain a sexual act, unwanted sexual comments or advances, or acts to traffic a person's sexuality, using coercion, threats of harm or physical force, by any person regardless of relationship to the victim, in any setting, including but not limited to home and work" (p. 149). Childhood sexual abuse (CSA) is defined as a sexual act between an adult or a minor with a child, in which the child is utilized for the sexual satisfaction of the perpetrator (Briere, 1992). Childhood sexual abuse is considered to be a traumatic event since the child is involved in sexual activity that he or she does not fully comprehend, is unable to give informed consent to, or for which the child is not developmentally prepared. As such, these acts violate the laws and/or social taboos of society.

The estimated prevalence of CSA across the world varies from 5% to 45%. This is due to methodological differences and varying definitions of CSA, as well as the questionable accuracy of figures citing childhood sexual abuse due to the inability to assume complete disclosure from children (Fergusson, Horwood, & Lynsky, 1997). Nonetheless, recent surveys revealed that CSA, as well as other forms of child abuse, is widespread. For example, recent US data from the National Child Abuse and Neglect Data System shows that among approximately 681,000 cases of child abuse and neglect that were investigated in 2011, 61,500 were cases of sexual abuse (Finkelhore et al., 2013). A nationwide prevalence study of child maltreatment in the Netherlands (NPM-2005), which replicated the NIS-4 methodology (Euser et al., 2010), found that 4% of Dutch children who were maltreated in 2005 experienced CSA. This statistic is lower than what had been found in a similar research study conducted in Australia (2010), which showed a rate of 4-8% for penetrative abuse and 12-16% for non-penetrative sexual abuse among males and a 7-12% for penetrative abuse and 23–36% for non-penetrative abuse among females. Another national survey of child maltreatment, carried out in the UK (Radford et al., 2010) via telephone, interviewed parents who reported a prevalence rate of 16.5% sexual abuse. A 2012 review of child sexual abuse prevalence in East Asia and the Pacific (Fry et al., 2012) revealed similar rates: sexual contact (ranging from 1.7% in Hong Kong to 11.6% in the Pacific Islands) and forced sexual intercourse (ranging from 13.8% in the Mariana Islands to 29.3% in the Marshall Islands). Recently, a national epidemiological survey conducted on 8,300 children and youth in Israel reported a prevalence rate of 17.8% of victims of sexual abuse, who had either been threatened with sexual penetration or experienced actual penetration (Lev-Wiesel & Eisikovits, 2013, unpublished).

There is clear scientific evidence showing that childhood sexual abuse has long term negative psychological effects contingent on variables such as the age of the victim at the onset of the abuse, the severity of violence inflicted upon the victimized child, the extent to which the sexual abuse was performed with "love, care, and tenderness," the duration of the abuse, the identity of the perpetrator, the form of the sexual abuse (exploitation, harassment, exposure to pornography, with or without penetration), the location of the occurrence (home vs. outside the home), and the victim's personal and social resources (e.g., Laaksonen et al., 2011). Detrimental mental health outcomes that have been consistently associated with childhood sexual abuse include post-traumatic symptoms (e.g., Canton-Cortes & Canton, 2010); depression (e.g., Fergusson et al., 2008); substance abuse (e.g., O'Leary & Gould, 2009); helplessness, negative attributions, aggressive behaviors and conduct, and eating disorders (Jonas et al., 2011); and anxiety (e.g., Banyard, Williams, & Siegel, 2001). More recently, childhood sexual abuse has also been linked to psychotic episodes including schizophrenia and delusional disorder (e.g., Bendall, Jackson, Hulbert, & McGorry, 2011) as well as personality disorders (Cutajar et al., 2010). Childhood sexual abuse involving penetration has been identified as a risk factor, in particular, and known to be associated with severe outcomes such as psychotic and schizophrenic syndromes (Cutajar et al., 2010).

In addition, dissociation, a mental process that produces a lack of connection in the person's thoughts, memories, feelings, actions, or sense of self (American Psychiatric Association, 1994), is both a short- and long-term effect of CSA. The victim unconsciously uses dissociative, defensive functions such as creating automatic behaviors, escaping from life stressors and despair, compartmentalizing catastrophic events, seeking cathartic relief from certain feelings, avoiding and relieving pain, and altering the sense of self so that the traumatic event is experienced as if "it hadn't happened" to them (Putnam, 1993). According to Silberg (1998), sexually abused children tend to dissociate themselves during a traumatic event. This state allows the child to survive and protect his or her functioning self as much as possible (Krystal et al., 2000; Midgley, 2002). Through this mechanism, abused children can temporarily avoid the full onslaught of their pain and suffering. Escaping the abusive situation can often be possible only virtually in the victim's mind, whereas the body continues to suffer (Silberg, 1998). As a result, through dissociation, victims are able to block out certain aspects of reality so they do not have to be fully aware of the devastating danger and pain they are actually experiencing. Indeed, if they were totally cognizant of their inescapable peril, it would likely overwhelm their mental processes. Dissociation permits the complete blocking out of reality in the effort to hold on to one's sanity. Unfortunately, continuous dissociation in childhood can lead to continued use of dissociative mechanisms and dissociative disorders in adulthood. These dissociations in adulthood cause confusion of the sense of self and identity, as well as problems in maintaining healthy relationships.

In an attempt to develop a systematic understanding of the outcomes of childhood sexual abuse, Finkelhor and Browne (1985) proposed a categorization of the effects of child sexual abuse including four traumagenic dynamics - traumatic sexualization, betrayal, stigmatization, and powerlessness. These dynamics were identified as the core of the psychological injury caused by the abuse and helped practitioners to make assessments of victimized children and to anticipate vulnerability factors. However, while some treatment protocols and procedures are widely accepted by practitioners in the field of child abuse due to having a solid theoretical basis as well as considerable anecdotal support for their clinical utility, the majority of the treatment models have no systematic theoretical foundation, and there is little evidence indicating their clinical effectiveness. This concern is further supported by the evidence that some children or adult survivors deteriorate even after completing treatments that have empirical support (Crowler & Love, 2000).

Chapter 2 - The Uniqueness of Childhood Sexual Abuse

Based on previous literature showing that childhood sexual abuse varies according to the contextual circumstances, the form of the abuse, consequences (symptoms and severity), and the extent to which the experience is perceived by the victim as traumatic, this book attempts to provide a conceptual model of childhood sexual abuse according to the five traumagenic constructs: soul's homelessness - dislocation of the mind from the body; captured in time - the present and future become reflections of the past; re-enactment of the abuse; the betrayal entrapment; and entrapped in a distorted intimacy. These dimensions are suggested to encompass the experience of childhood sexual abuse and to provide useful heuristic devices to conceptualize it. They will be described and analyzed next, by using existing evidence from the literature.

Soul's Homelessness

There is a common belief that one's home is one's shelter. It provides safety and predictability, and as such, it is experienced as a point of departure and a landing pad. Similarly, one's body is perceived by humans to be their soul's home, and as such, the body is attributed the characteristics of a home. One's body is the point zero from which the experience of close, far, inner and outer are derived. The body is the soul's private space. Evidence indicates that people exhibit strong physical and emotional reactions to personal space violations (Kennedy, Gläscher, Tyszka, & Adolphs, 2009) that are produced by the amygdalae, particularly if the intimate zone reserved for loved ones is invaded. People view their personal space serving as a buffer vis-à-vis the external world, and it is essential that they experience control and responsibility over it (Hall, 1966). For example, a baby who refuses to be fed shuts his/her mouth and turns his/her head away from the nipple. The feeder, then, can use persuasion by arousal of the lips to the touch of the nipple or force the baby to open his or her mouth, which might cause the baby to vomit, suffocate or finally surrender. Sexually penetrating a child's body means breaking into the child's personal space, invading the child's intimate zone. This violation of the child's body destroys the child's sense of security and trust in the body, and calls into question the body's ability to defend itself and the soul it houses.

When a person's home is broken into by force and the sense of safety is threatened, the resident who experienced this trespass can move to another space, define it as home, and experience a renewed sense of security. In the case of a violation of a child's private space through bodily penetration, the option of identifying an alternative private and safe space is remote, and the immediate experience is that the body is no longer the metaphoric shelter of the soul but rather transformed into the soul's prison.

The relationship between body and soul historically was not viewed as harmonious. For instance, Plato viewed the relationship between body and soul (soma and psyche) as conflictual and unfortunate. The soul, according to Plato, is a helpless prisoner in the body, compelled to view reality only directly (Ogden, 1928, Phaedo 82d). Others, with comparable ideas, called the body a tomb of the soul (The Oxford Classical Dictionary, 1970, p. 895). In contrast, according to Biblical thought, the human body and soul are both sacred and created by God; they can and must function in harmony to fulfill God's purpose in the world. Emotion, intellect and body are all integral components of a human being, and there is no opposition between body and soul or flesh and spirit (Urbach, 1979). When the soul is imprisoned and abandoned, it has no escape and the damage is commensurate with its importance for existence. Thus, regardless of understandable reasons of why the body surrendered to the perpetrator, including being overwhelmed by anxiety (loss of control over the sphincters), physical inferiority, or being in a state of frightened immobility, once the body failed to defend the soul, devastating consequences can be expected in the survivor's existential experience as a whole. This failure to ward off the perpetrator is experienced as the body's betrayal of the soul - defined as a form of deception or dismissal of prior life assumptions, a breaking or violation of a presumptive psychological and social contract (trust, or confidence). This is likely to result in a conflict between the soul and body which produces a split in the individual's existence. The repulsive, uncontrolled, contaminated, traitor body deserves to be punished. However, being imprisoned within the body and forced to continue relying on it for mere survival, the soul can choose between three options. The first option, the soul can identify with the aggressor by taking onto itself the perpetrator role (often a long time after the abuse has ceased). The second option, the soul splits itself away from the body through employment of dissociation and ignoring the bodily needs, or, the third option, the soul can retaliate by punishing the body for its betrayal. Each option can be manifested in a variety of symptoms on a continuum of severity from suicidal attempts, self-injurious behaviors, substance abuse, eating disorders, promiscuity, and addiction to sadomasochistic sexual activities, to neglect of hygiene, depression, feelings of emptiness, etc.

Captured in Time

People can be described as time travelers: they draw on past memories, experience the present and look forward to the future (Zimbardo & Boyd, 1999). The way these journeys in time are integrated in experience makes a crucial difference to how well they do in life and how content and satisfied they are (Carstensen, 2006). In that respect, time perspectives — whether the person tends to get stuck in the past, live only for the moment, or is enslaved by ambitions concerning the future — are good predictors of educational and career success, general health, and happiness (Eckhart, 1999, Kauffman & Husman, 2004). Survivors of child sexual abuse often report among other symptoms intrusive thoughts and memories, flashbacks (sensory memories) and trance episodes (e.g., Roth, Newman, Pelcovitz, Van Der Kolk, & Mandel, 1997) as a result of the trauma (e.g., Briere, 1992). Survivors may re-experience the trauma mentally and physically when they experience cues or triggers associated with the previous traumatic events; at times these occurrences cause re-traumatization (Carlson & Ruzek, 2005). When re-experiencing the trauma, occasionally, survivors feel they will not be able to be released from their past. As a result, feelings of despair, loss of self-esteem, and depression are heightened. In the sense that they re-experience the trauma, often, the victims' present and future become reflections of the past. It is not surprising, therefore, that victims tend to view life situations and relationships through the prism of the abuse and their previous relationship with the abuser (trust, danger, etc.).

The life of the victimized child revolves around the abuse, waiting before it occurs, during and waiting for the next abusive event after it happens. In this respect, the abuse and life become one; the abuse is the only real certainty to come. The figure/ground phenomenon alters their perception in a manner that the real, external life (outside the abuse, such as school and friends) is felt as unreal – whereas the abusive experience becomes the only reality; the ever domineering background is the abuse; as a result, the symptom of de-realization develops.

Time perspective refers to the sense of time, which differs from other senses since it cannot be directly perceived, but it is reconstructed by the brain. Humans can perceive relatively short periods of time in milliseconds and also durations that are a significant fraction of a lifetime. Human perception of time duration is subjective, termed by Minkowski as "dure" (Minkowski, 1933). Data indicate that the sense of time as duration (time as it is felt) develops by early infancy, while time as perspective (time as a concept) develops by late infancy or early toddlerhood. Investigators (e.g., Butler, 1999) propose that the sense of time develops out of perception of bodily function and is intimately related to the development of the sense of self. The sense of time further evolves as a function of psychosexual and other developmental stages. Not surprisingly, therefore, the younger the victim of sexual abuse is, the more severe the time-dependent outcomes in terms of psychosocial symptomatology and health (e.g., Briere, 1997).

Time Cycling

A childhood sexual abuse event is an intense and extremely stressful situation in which the time is likely to be experienced by the victim as infinite. When this event becomes continual, the child learns to identify the signs of the impending occurrence, to recognize the highest hit point in the momentary immediate event, and the signals indicating that the specific traumatic occurrence came to an end. When the perpetrator leaves, whether or not the child is physically injured, physical relief emerges - a sensation of natural relaxation (the body releases chemicals, muscles relax, the heart rate slows down, and blood flow to the brain increases) due to an experiential distancing from the source of stress (the perpetrator). However, this relaxation does not last long. Anxiety and fear gradually increase due to decrease of the dissociation mechanisms employed during the event itself, and dreading the next inevitable frightening encounter with the abuser. Thus, the child is circling from dreading the inevitable encounter with the abuser, experiencing the abuse, relief when it temporally ends, to re-dreading the next abusive event. This creates a psychological construct of being entrapped in time, and is exhibited as being disoriented in time (Drake, Duncan, Sutherland, Abernethy & Henry, 2008). In addition, victims of childhood sexual abuse often suffer from various forms of distorted experiential time manifested in symptoms such as trance, persistent dissociation, and loss of time.

Entrapped in Distorted Intimacy

Some of the repercussions of incestuous relationship, specifically father-daughter incest, include a marked sense of isolation from the family (Weinberg, 1955), difficulty to control anger, problems in forming and maintaining trusting relationships, and inability to establish intimate relationships with people other than the perpetrator (Seidman, Marshall, Hudson, & Robertson, 1994). Courtois (1999) suggested that the impact of incest is highly subjective and, thus, not easily predicted from mere knowledge of the circumstances (duration, repetition of the abuse, age at onset, etc.). In a meta-analysis of studies focusing on incest, Rind and Tromovitch (1997) generated controversy by suggesting that childhood sexual abuse does not always cause pervasive harm, that some college students reported such encounters as positive experiences and that the extent of psychological damage depends on whether or not the child described the encounter as consensual. Evidence indicated that the father-daughter distorted intimacy is often encouraged, tolerated or denied by other members of the family including the mothers (Seidman et al., 1994). Incestuous daughters are sometimes eager to assume adult roles, and gratified by their fathers' attention.

An incestuous relationship involves self-disclosure and self-revealing of unacceptable fantasies, behaviors, sexual arousal, feelings of fear, shame and horror, negative closeness and interdependence between the parties involved, whereas normative intimacy involves self-disclosure, positive affection, closeness, and interdependence between the involved partners (Doweny, 2001). The victimized child naturally internalizes a distorted model of intimacy, which harms his or her future abilities to establish fulfilling intimacy, which leads to loneliness, depression, lower self-esteem, anxiety, and less relational satisfaction (Pielage, Luteijn, & Arrindell, 2005). Since intimacy is a vital human need for mental health and psychosocial adjustment (Descutner & Thelen, 1991), and close intimate relationships are the most important source for individual well-being and a sense of meaning in life (Bartholomew, 1990; Pielage, et al., 2005), the survivor is likely to either yearn to reestablish the past distorted intimate relationships, reenact the distorted intimacy with others, or avoid any close relationships. Symptoms such as addiction to pornography and involvement in sadomasochistic sexual activities often occur. Based on clinical observations, it can be assumed that the greater the emotional ambivalence towards the perpetrator, the greater the entrapment in the distorted intimacy is likely to be.

Fear of intimacy is likely to be acquired as a trait which later might inhibit the capacity to exchange thoughts and feelings of personal significance due to anxiety. Survivors who fear intimacy desire interpersonal closeness but fear rejection, and, thus, experience anxiety during verbal and non-verbal communication with others. Other important elements in the fear of intimacy include the denial of the need for intimacy, a fear of becoming dependent on others, and a dishonest posture of macho invulnerability (Firestone & Catlett, 1999).

From a psychodynamic perspective, having been involved in such a distorted intimacy, being played as a puppet by the perpetrator, having the perpetrator as the key significant other from an early age, is bound to severely affect the victim's self-identity and self-esteem. The victimized child internalizes the perpetrator figure, including its psychological characteristics, and often imitates the perpetrator's style and voice. The perpetrator becomes part of the victim's internal world. The boundaries between the perpetrator and the child are blurred as the boundaries between the real and unreal, right and wrong, become gradually more and more permeable. The victimized child embodies two roles, the helpless, suffering victim and the strong, domineering perpetrator. When the abuse is prolonged and repeated, separation-individuation cannot be accomplished. As a result, the ability for authenticity diminishes. The victimized child is caught in a world of pseudo- appreciation, visibility and acknowledgement by the perpetrator who has become the main pillar of a distorted world. Hirsch (1996) claimed that psychological coping with severe traumatic aggression in the family can be handled by identification with, acceptance of, and submission to the overwhelming power.

The victim interjects the terror, identifies himself with it, and so remains victim throughout his life by repetition compulsion. Anna Freud (1936) coined the term "identification with the aggressor" - defined as an unconscious process in which a person adopts the perspective or behavior patterns of a captor or abuser. Along the same lines, abused children tend to show more ego-strength and the ability to defend themselves aggressively; they have attacked their fear by identifying with it. According to Freud (1936), this is a defense mechanism used to "protect the self from hurt and disorganization." The child learns to reduce his or her anxiety by changing from the passive to the active role. This is one possible explanation of why abused children become abusive adults or develop complex PTSD and dissociative disorders (D'Andrea, Ford, Stolbach, Spinazzola, & Van der Kolk, 2012).

The need to adapt and function in contrasting realities (the secret abusive world vs. the external world), in addition to being subjected to a prolonged repetitive trauma, was found to often result in developing dissociative disorders (Schalinski, Elbert & Schauer, 2011). Being under the control of the perpetrator, unable to flee, forces the ego to disintegrate into fragments in order to preserve some healthy functions (Jennings & Armsworth, 1992). Through classic and operant conditioning, the child learns that dissociation helps to survive the abuse, thus, gradually, dissociative disorders, including dissociative identity disorder, develop.

The Betrayal Entrapment

Betrayal is the violation of expressed or perceived trust by a person or persons on whom the individual relies upon for some aspect of his/her life. In the case of childhood sexual abuse, whether or not the perpetrator is an acquaintance or a stranger, a peer or a family member, if it was expected or not, the sexual abuse is a betrayal in the basic belief that the world is a place where children are protected from evil. Children naturally perceive adults as their guides and protectors and their home as a safe haven and a shelter. When the perpetrator is a family member and other family members ignore or encourage the abuse, the child loses trust and confidence in the significant others (such as parental figures) as well as in the belief that the world is a safe place. However, not only the direct perpetrators are perceived to betray the child's trust, the external systems, such as teachers, friends, and extended family, are perceived as traitors as well. Even if the child does not disclose or hint to them about his/her personal distress, his/her natural expectation is that adults in general, and those who are supposed to care in particular, such as teachers, will see and understand the situation.

Jennifer Freyd (1996) was the first to use the term "betrayal trauma" to explain why victims might repress the memories of harmful experiences inflicted upon them by a person on whom they rely. Substantially similar to the theory of dissociative amnesia, the theory of betrayal trauma (DePrince, et al., 2012) proposes that social utility might cause an individual to undergo traumatic amnesia in favor of maintenance of a relationship perceived as needed for survival. Unawareness and forgetting of abuse were substantially higher when the relationship between perpetrator and victim involved closeness, trust, or care-giving. Hensley (2009c) defines betrayal trauma as biopsychosocial harm caused by an actual or perceived violation of a psychological contract by person(s) upon whom the victim relies for some aspect of his or her well-being. Hensley (2009c) argues that betrayal trauma is far more injurious than physical and other traumas, because it destabilizes the mental model, schemas, and psychological contracts the victim has established in order to see, understand, and respond to life events, and thus causes extreme biopsychosocial distress as a result. It violates the victim's understanding of rules, roles, relationships, respect, morals, ethics, and values, which are the core tenets of the psychological contract. A return to equilibrium requires the individual to redefine one or more of these tenets.

However, the abused child might also perceive himself/herself as a betrayer. In cases in which the perpetrator is a close family member, as time passes from the onset of abuse and nothing is reported, the victim's feelings of guilt concerning the abuse increase. The mere participation in the sexual interaction can be perceived as collaboration in an unacceptable relationship. Clearly, it becomes more difficult when the victim has feelings of love toward the perpetrator, or the victim feels unique and chosen by receiving the perpetrator's affections. These situations increase the child's feelings of guilt on the one hand and the feelings of being special on the other. Further, the mere need or will to reveal the secret is experienced as a betrayal. The betrayal deserves punishment; the betrayer deserves to be punished, if not by others, by oneself.

An additional aspect to the betrayal entrapment stems from the body's betrayal of the mind and soul. As already mentioned in the previous section, Soul's Homelessness, victims of sexual abuse feel that the body has betrayed the soul, even if they, the victim, were powerless against the perpetrator. Moreover, if the body responded with sexual arousal during the sexually abusive event, this response causes feelings of repulsiveness and rejection of the physical body by the soul. The soul does not want to continue living in the body. In these situations, the response to the body's betrayal of the soul ranges from total disregard of the body, as expressed in symptoms like eating disorders, addictions, neglect of hygiene, and avoiding physical needs, to deliberate and severe self-injurious behavior, such as self-cutting and suicidal acts.

A major consequence of the overall betrayal is the loss of the ability to be authentic across situations. The child learns to survive in a world filled with double messages: Do not lie, but do not tell the truth. Sex is forbidden, but hidden sex is allowed. Love is painful. Parents are an unsafe shelter. Life dimensions are disconnected from one another and energy is invested in protecting information traveling from one dimension to the other. Different personas appear or disappear according to the life situation. Like an actor on a stage who plays all the roles, so too does the victimized child, especially in a family where incest occurs. In these situations, the child does not have the opportunity to be himself. In each dimension, he must become someone else as required by others. In childhood, the personality is still developing, but these situations cause the victim to constantly perform different roles and reduce his/her ability to authentically experiment with roles, a requirement for healthy development. The opportunity to become himself/herself is ripped away from the child.

The ability to answer that is denied as the boundaries between who the victim is and who he/she needs to be are blurred. In addition, the victim performs in context of a larger than life number of "provinces of meaning" (a term used by Alfred Shutz in Hindess, 1972). As in the theater, the curtain is up and a whole other world appears. The victim enters, then the curtain goes down and the victim is expected to go back to the real world. But is there a real world? Such changes are the source of much instability and insecurity that along with loss of authenticity lead to severe identity liability.

Authenticity is the basis for intimacy, defined as the ability of a person to share his/her deepest feelings and weakness with another and the ability to feel empathy for another. The lack of authenticity prevents the victim from building an intimate relationship that is not distorted with another person. This lack of intimacy increases the victim's loneliness and aloneness throughout his/her lifetime. Thus, betrayal at any stage of the socio-developmental cycle results in extreme biopsychosocial distress reaching far beyond the event itself. It disrupts the person's established mental model by which he or she views, understands, and responds to his or her environment and life events. The betrayal also destabilizes the psychological contracts by which one trusts, and negates important aspects of viable strategies by which the person copes with life events (Hensley, 2009c) and by which a person can live in peace with oneself.

Reenactment

One of the negative results for children who are sexually abused by someone with power, authority, or greater physical size, is that the developing child does not learn appropriate boundaries. What seems "normal" to a sexually abused child is to surrender not only their body, but also their thoughts, feelings, and beliefs (compliance). Reenactments of boundary violations are quite common and occur for a variety of reasons whether intentional (consciously) or unintentional (unconsciously; Levy, 1998). Van der Kolk and Greenberg (1987) claimed that childhood sexual abuse can lead to ego deficits that render an individual susceptible to both reenactments and re-victimization as a result of their addiction to trauma (Russel 1986). Chu (1998) posited that reenacting a past trauma is a way an individual attempts to master it, yet, lifelong reenactments and re-exposure to trauma rarely result in resolution and mastery. Reenactments caused by rigidified defenses lead to reenactments of the problems that the original defenses sought to avoid. The effort to master the trauma is a maladaptive mechanism and the strategy results in continued distress and difficulties for the individual. One of the factors found to contribute to the frequent reenactments of trauma of survivors is the use of dissociative defenses (Van der Kolk & McFarlane, 1996).

Reenactments following childhood sexual abuse are presented in forms of self-harming behaviors, actively reenacting a past trauma, and/or abuse of others. In adult survivors, self-harming behavior in the form of active reenactments of childhood sexual trauma can be more reflective of a maladaptive defensive posture than an adaptive process (Kaufman & Zigler, 1989). According to Van der Kolk (1989), self-injurious behaviors perpetuate the stress-relaxation cycle by producing the stress related opioid stimulation.

Van der Kolk and Van der Hart (1989) posited that survivors of childhood sexual abuse are addicted to the trauma and, therefore, may try to recreate it due to overstimulation of sexualization (i.e., a victim of childhood sexual abuse may become a prostitute). Such individuals have reported feeling bored, apprehensive, and anxious when not experiencing some form of activity reminiscent of their trauma. It can be suggested that this need for stress arousal can be an impetus for reenactment behaviors. For children who experience trauma, these experiences became synonymous with relationships, and the child is often in a constant state of arousal due to fear, rage, hyperalertness, or anxiety. This constant arousal impacts the child's biochemistry and inhibits a return to a baseline. Thus, as an adult, the individual may be addicted to an excitement which is painful, but at the same time he/she finds this excitement pleasurable and comfortable. Further, Van der Kolk and Van der Hart (1989) reported that high levels of stress activate the physiological opioid systems. Just as heroin may activate this system and create a cycle of dependence and withdrawal, so might the hyperarousal that is created with trauma.

Salter et al. (2003) explains that a victim who reenacts the abuse by becoming an active abuser takes the abuser role as a defensive stance. In the abuser role, the victim reenacts the past, but ensures that he/she will not re-experience the terror and helplessness related to the old traumatic situation or relationship. In addition, the abusive act allows the individual to express and direct rage at others (Lalor & McElvaney, 2010).

An additional aspect for reenactment could stem from the desire to re-experience the momentary relief experienced when the abuser releases the victim and leaves the scene. During the time of the trauma, endorphin levels remain elevated and help numb the emotional and physical pain of the trauma. However, after the trauma is over, endorphin levels gradually decrease and this may lead to a period of endorphin withdrawal that can last from hours to days. This period of endorphin withdrawal may initially be felt as a relief, but it gradually produces emotional distress and contributes to other symptoms of posttraumatic stress disorder (Volpicelli, Balaraman, Hahn, Wallace, & Bux, 1999). Thus, the brief sensation of physical and emotional relief acts as a reward to the traumatic event, and might become an addictive factor in reenactment.

Chapter 3 - Assessment and Treatment of CSA

One of the problems clinicians face during therapy with adults is the diagnosis of sexually abused survivors, since there are no physical symptoms to attest to the abuse. Jones (1990) pointed out that physical symptoms are rarely seen among sexually abused children, so the condition is diagnosed in childhood and/or adulthood according to behavioral and emotional symptoms such as self-destructive behavior (Sedney & Brooks, 1984; Young, 1990), learning and employment difficulties (Lisak & Luster, 1994), difficulties in sexual relationships, changes in mood, loneliness and depression (Berliner, Blick & Bulkley, 1981), fantasy (Riggs, 1982), and feelings of guilt and fear. All these symptoms are accompanied by shame about the traumatic experience.

Evaluation and diagnosis of childhood sexual abuse in drawings has mainly gathered in clinical settings (e.g., DiLeo, 1996) which raised the question of validity. However, several studies have indicated some differences in human figures drawn by survivors of sexual abuse compared to children and adults who did not have a history of childhood abuse. For example, Chantler, Pelco and Mertin (1993) who compared the drawings of human figures done by two groups of children, CSA victims vs. non-

CSA victims, found that cut-off hands, clinging or incomplete arms, poor integration of body parts, and absence of legs were significantly more frequent among sexually abused children. Lev-Wiesel (1999) who compared incestuous vs. non-sexually abused female adults' self-figure drawings found four indicators that significantly differ between the two groups: eyes (hollowed, shadowed or omitted), arms and hands (hanging, disconnected or omitted), chin or cheek (emphasized or doubled), and lower body either shadowed or disconnected/omitted from upper body. It is important to note that assessment of the trauma is part of the therapeutic process since it allows the client to feel that the therapist can and is willing to contain his/her life story.

In order for the therapeutic process to become a corrective experience, the elements of the sexual abuse should be used to lead towards growth rather than towards re-captivity. Corrective experience is defined as an experience that is similar to the past traumatic experience in regard to the main issue, but totally different in regard to the way it is conducted, the relationship itself and the consequences. Corrective experience in terms of cradling the victimized child without the time and intensity dimensions that symbolically parallel the abusive experience might unintentionally entrap both the therapist and the client. The helpless victim who needs protection is the main player in the drama. He lures the therapist to the cage of entrapment as the therapist plays the role of the protector, like the Pied Piper. The client's need for warmth and containment from the therapist and his/her fear of abandonment might cause him/her to preserve his/her role as helpless and needy. The interjected perpetrator figure might paradoxically appear as a victim who needs constant assistance and protection. Even an experienced therapist might experience a savior fantasy that is likely to encourage the client to maintain his/her role as a victim. Both the therapist and the client therefore will preserve the entrapment state, only in reversed roles, without awareness of their covert roles, the victimized client as the hunter and the warm therapist as the prisoner. A therapist and a client who are caught in such a relationship that recreates the entrapment without awareness have positive feelings towards the therapeutic process itself and towards each other. The result of not being aware of the activation of this pattern will be a long-term therapeutic relationship with parental expressions of love and protection through years of therapy.

It is imperative that therapists of sexual abuse survivors will ask themselves during each phase of the therapeutic process the following questions: Is the sexual abuse the client's dominant problem? Is the sexual abuse traumatic? What was the cause of the trauma during the experience? What is the meaning of the sexual abuse for the victim? What is the meaning of the perpetrator for the victim? What are the symptoms? What is the main symptom? What does it represent? What is the secret the client hides from himself? Who are the internal voices and what do they say? Who are the significant figures and what are their main messages to the client? What is the weight of each message? What personal and social resources does the client have? What does the therapist represent to the client? What type of transference occurs between both the client and the therapist? What does the therapist feel toward the client? What is the therapist reluctant to hear? What are the therapist's body sensations, feelings, and thoughts that are aroused in the presence of the client? What does the client dare not say to the therapist and why? In addition to continuous clinical supervision, answering these questions might help to detect projective identification processes and pathological patterns, such as recreating the entrapment.

It is the therapist's role to help the client experience posttraumatic growth. Posttraumatic growth means growing out of pain and loss, despite pain and loss, and coexisting with pain and loss (Lev-Wiesel, Amir, Besser, 2005). Posttraumatic growth does not mean erasing the event or forgiving. Posttraumatic growth is defined as a change in three dimensions. The first is a change in self-perception, meaning the victim feels more vulnerable yet strong and has coping abilities. The second dimension is the change in the perception of relationships, meaning the greater ability to be more intimate and close, less pretending, a greater sense of compassion and a deep understanding that time is a limited, precious resource. The third dimension is a change in life philosophy, meaning broadening alternatives in any life domain, a change of priorities, and a greater appreciation of the little things in life.

In order for the victim to allow himself/herself to express the contradicting feelings towards significant figures, particularly in cases of incest, and the ability to share intimate details from the abuse itself, the client must feel that the therapist is ready to contain, accept and be strong in the face evil, pain, suffering, helplessness, loss as well as support, love and longing for the perpetrator. It is necessary that the therapy will become a corrective experience in terms of creating non-abusive intimacy with an adult, a safe place compared to the dangerous, fearful place of the past. This safe, intimate relationship with an adult allows the client to change his/her perception of relationships.

The sexual abuse event is an intensive experience in terms of the precise time (minutes, hours, months, years). In order to survive, dissociative mechanisms are activated, often developing into dissociative disorders. The normative therapeutic setting is usually limited to approximately an hour or two once or twice week. Therefore, there is a high probability that dissociation will be activated between one session and the next. Practically, the pauses between sessions can cause clients to regress to the starting point. For example, talking about a painful memory during a single session will probably cause overwhelming feelings of anxiety, rage, or agony both during and after the session terminated. This emotional overwhelming will automatically activate the dissociative mechanisms, which will in turn cause repression, amnesia, physical and emotional detachment and distancing from that memory. The emotionally overwhelmed client will arrive to the following session in a different, possibly detached, state that will not allow him/ her to reenter the pain. This creates a cycle of returning to the starting point, again and again. Despite the fact that the client perceives the therapy as a safe place, unintentionally, it might strengthen the uncontrollable activation of dissociative mechanisms which in turn will prevent or postpone healing. The client will remain in a state of survival and resilience rather than finding posttraumatic growth in the therapy (see the hourglass in Ziv's drawings and her perception of time).

In addition, the time framework and intensiveness of therapy of sexual abuse survivors has a psychodynamic meaning. It can be seen in the intensiveness of the dialogue between the therapist and Ziv. Using technology and breaking the normative, acceptable framework of therapy (hour and place) did not allow Ziv to use extensive dissociation; thus, regression was prevented. Ziv only used dissociation when she was overwhelmed with unbearable pain or terror or fear for short periods of time in order to rest and reenergize. The progress occurred in a type of spiral process in which each cycle consisted of a step-by-step approach to painful material - bringing up new details or memories, overwhelming, detachment, resting, and beginning a new cycle. The cycles always moved Ziv forward in a spiral movement. From cycle to cycle, the times in between were shortened; the resting times were shortened. The forward movement enabled Ziv to have new insights. Physical, emotional and cognitive processes became integrated. The need to use dissociation decreased with time. Ziv's feeling of safety while coping with both socially acceptable and unacceptable feelings (according to her perception) and her readiness to watch and analyze herself as a child and as an adult, to face its consequences, her ability to cope with her deepest fears, such as abandonment and loneliness, were strengthened. The essence of the spiral process is moving forward toward growth through combining physical, emotional and cognitive mechanisms.

Chapter 4 - Using Drawings within Therapy

Therapists, particularly art therapists, have long emphasized the unique role of nonverbal techniques within the clinical setting. Nonverbal therapeutic techniques involve invoking kinesthetic and visual cues to memories and mental images, thereby gaining access to suppressed emotions. Such techniques also provide the benefits of creativity and spontaneity, which serve to ameliorate and counteract feelings of hopelessness and worthlessness in the patient.

Current research lends support to the idea that the body may remember traumatic experiences even when the mind appears to have forgotten them. A number of recent studies focusing on the biology of post-traumatic stress disorder (PTSD) indicated that there are persistent and profound alternations in stress hormone secretion and memory processing in patients suffering from this disturbance (Van der Kolk, 1999; Yehuda, Mcfarlane & Shalev, 1998). It has also been demonstrated that through art, access may be gained to implicit memory systems and visual-kinesthetic schemata usually processed by the predominantly nonverbal right hemisphere of the brain (Johnson, 2000).

Based on my own (R. Lev-Wiesel) and other researchers'

clinical observations (e.g. Derek, 1989; Forward, 1990), it would appear that the stronger the patient's feelings of self-blame, shame, anger, and doubt in his or her ability to maintain self-control, the more difficulty he or she has in talking about past traumatic experiences. These feelings are particularly strong among people who have suffered violence at the hands of members of their own family, on whom they lean and trust. Through my work as a family and group therapist, I have found that drawing often helps adults and children who have survived domestic violence to express the sensations, feelings, and thoughts associated with the trauma. Drawing also seems to help to reconstruct and reorganize the painful experience, allowing the client to acquire a sense of control over the intrusive thoughts, memories, and overwhelming negative feelings (e.g., fear and hate) towards the offenders. As a result, the ability of the client to verbalize their experiences and feelings improves.

An additional advantage of using drawing as a clinical tool is that drawings can assist therapists in detecting clients' consciously or unconsciously hidden conflicts and traumata which they may be reluctant to raise within the therapeutic setting. Survivors of domestic violence, particularly children who have undergone sexual abuse, are often hesitant to discuss their experience with a stranger – even if that stranger is a therapist. This reluctance occurs for a variety of reasons, such as uncertainty as to whether the abuse really occurred, or the need to obtain the therapist's approval before relating the experience (often because a promise of secrecy has been forced upon them previously by the offender).

Many current theories in the interpretation of drawings have evolved largely from ideas generated in the work of Jung (1964) who emphasized the importance of symbols and the way they manifest their significance through drawings from the unconscious. Bach (1969) demonstrated that the unconscious contents in drawings could be deciphered psychologically. Furth (1988) pointed out that a systematic analysis of drawings, very similar to dream analysis, can further understanding and awareness of messages from the unconscious. Analytic interpretation of the expressions in the drawing, revealing one's weaknesses, fears, and negative traits, as well as one's strengths, accomplishments and untapped potential, gives insight into who one is. Unconscious material originating in the psyche will remain in the psyche while manifesting itself externally in outer world difficulties. These difficulties and adaptations appear symbolically in drawings or in dreams. Following the symbol, a person approaches the complex in which the problem is woven, thus allowing the energy connected to the complex to flow. Since the energy can no longer remain stagnant, it begins to flow as the person encounters it, and it can then be brought to consciousness (Furth, 1988).

Projective drawings are obtained in an encounter between two individuals who must form some sort of relationship with each other, however brief. There are two primary situations in which drawings are used by clinicians: (1) as a projective technique, which is usually done by a diagnostician, someone other than an ongoing therapist, and as a one-time activity, and (2) in art therapy, in which a relationship develops of the same kind as one engendered in any other form of ongoing therapy. Information on the use of drawings in a psychotherapeutic context is scarce, although projective techniques such as the Draw-A-Person (Machover, 1949), the House-Tree-Person (Buck, 1966), and Kinetic Family (Burns & Kaufman, 1972) exercises are used often by therapists mostly for diagnostic purposes. Furth (1988) pointed out that a series of drawings with all their focal points must be assessed before a diagnostic or prognostic evaluation is possible.

Draw a Person Test

The Machover Draw-A-Person (DAP) test is one of the most frequently used assessment instruments (Pihl & Nimrod, 1976). Both intellectual and emotional functioning are purported to be measured by this seemingly uncomplicated test. Machover (1949) developed the DAP test as a measure of personality. It is based on the theory that the drawn figure is the subject, and that the paper represents the subject's environment. Of particular interest is the linking of special meaning to specific body parts. Through this link the drawings may be used to assist in identifying somatic and psychological problems. The request "draw a person" allows the patient to choose freely the age, sex, stance, action and expression of the figure. The drawer shows the figure according to his/her deep acquaintance with himself/herself.

Overall, interpreting the DAP test includes the study of four major body areas:
1. **The head** is considered to be the locus of the sense of self or the ego. The eyes and the ears receive stimuli or extra-personal data. The mouth serves as an inlet for taking things into the body and as an outlet for aggression, friendliness, and other feelings. The head is considered to provide the examiner with the most valid insight into the subject's interaction with others as well as his/her self-concept.
2. **The hands, arms, shoulders, and chest** combine to form a functional unit to execute the commands of the brain or the impulses of the body. The examiner should note the size, shape, and strength which may indicate the degree of reaching out, aggression, and conflictual areas.
3. **The torso/trunk of the body** indicates strength features similar to those of the hands, arms, shoulders and chest. Here the clothing covers the body and is important symbolically as the facade which subjects present the world.
4. **Legs and feet** are considered to symbolize autonomy, self-movement, self-direction, and balance.

The interaction of the four major body areas is vital in order to accurately evaluate the drawing. The goal in the evaluation is to identify the areas of conflict, exaggeration, omission, and distortion. Examiners also should take into consideration the subject's background, family structure, and spontaneous comments during the drawing process, particularly comments regarding lack of control (Abraham, 1989; Furth, 1988; Hammer, 1997; Koppitz, 1968).

Based on children's drawings, Koppitz (1968) developed three different categories (30 items) in order to distinguish human figure indicators between those who suffer emotional difficulties and those who do not. The first category includes items reflecting the quality of the drawing (poor integration of parts, shading of face, shading of body and/or limbs, shading of hands and/or neck, gross asymmetry of limbs, figure slanting by 15 degrees or more, tiny figure, big figure, and transparencies). The second category includes: tiny head, crossed eyes, teeth, short arms, long arms, arms clinging to side of body, hands as big as head, hands cut off, legs pressed together, genitals, monster or grotesque figure, three or more figures spontaneously drawn, and clouds or rain. The third category includes the omission of eight basic items which can normally be expected in a human figure drawing (no eyes; no nose; no body; no mouth; no arms; no legs; no feet; no neck).

Lakin's (1956) use of the DAP test with the elderly and adolescents found that the drawings that the elderly created revealed the feeling of shrinking in contrast to the adolescents' drawings that showed the feeling of expanding. In another study, Johnson (1989) pointed out that hearing problems among deaf children appear in their human figure drawings through distorted, enlarged or omitted ears.

Some doubts have been raised about the validity of the DAP test (Blum, 1954), because of the techniques used to test reliability and validity (Pihl & Nimrod, 1976). Abraham (1989) argued that personality rather than arbitrary circumstances will determine the drawing process. This argument is supported by Graham's (1956) findings that after teaching students the meaning of their human figure drawings, their next drawings expressed the same indications as the previous ones. However, empirical research showed that DAP test correlated significantly with the Guilford-Zimmerman Temperament Survey (Cull & Hardy, 1971), Anxiety Indices (Johnson, 1971; Sopchak, 1970), and measures of depression and emotional disturbances (Koppitz, 1968; Glutting & Nester, 1986; Halinova, McLeodova & Sulcova, 1987; Johnson, 1989).

Use of Drawings in Treating Sexual Abuse Survivors

Sexual abuse means harming the physical body. Van der Kolk (1994) claimed that traumatic event is registered in the brain, meaning that which causes the body to respond similarly to the way it responded during the traumatic event; when current internal and external stimulus are associated with the past traumatic event, the body responds automatically in arousal or freezes often similarly to the same response that occurred during the event itself. Van der Kolk (1994) called this reaction "the body keeps the score." The bodily injury, even if it is not seen externally, is experienced physically. Sexual abuse survivors, as well as survivors of other traumas, often say they cannot verbally describe their traumatic experience because it is beyond description. The scenes, the feelings, the emotions are beyond verbal limits. Creative means such as drawing, movement, drama, or music enable expressions since they combine the different senses.

The use of drawing as a tool to express conscious and unconscious conflicts bypasses the body's defensive mechanisms by utilizing the existing dissociative mechanisms; it encourages and strengthens the verbal expressions of the victim. The younger the victim was at the time of the trauma, the more limited his/her verbal abilities and his/her coping resources (such as hardiness, sense of coherence, and sense of potency). There is a greater need in these cases to use creative means that will enable the victim to describe the story by using the body. Drawing in this sense is a physical activity; the hand movement creates symbols (shape, color, size, and placement). Studies (e.g., Machover, 1949) have shown that the symbols presented in the drawings that relate to the traumatic event precede the child's cognitive insight. Later, awareness of these symbols enables the child to continue to acquire additional insights and understanding which are necessary for posttraumatic growth and change (Lev-Wiesel, 1999).

The description of the painful memories or parts of it, including interjected figures, such as the perpetrator himself/herself, can be presented through the drawings. Also, drawings often contain additional figure or similar symbols that, counted together, indicate the age in which the traumatic event had been experienced. Findings of a study that investigated the richness of narratives given by children who lived in the shadow of a parent with drug-addiction (Lev-Wiesel & Raz, 2007) indicated that the children who were first asked to draw their life with the addicted parent added feelings and emotions to the facts in their narratives, compared to children of drug addicts who did not draw, but were only asked to give a narrative. The verbal ability and the readiness to share negative feelings such as suffering and pain increase significantly following the drawing session.

These findings strengthen theoretical models focusing on attitudes as a concept. Every attitude consists of three aspects: emotional, cognitive and behavioral. The emotional aspect is primary and is the foundation of the cognitive and behavioral aspects.

Additional comments:

1. Art therapy is relatively similar to the therapeutic process using dreams; beyond the overt plot, unconscious conflict is hidden and disguised by the different symbols that arise in the art.
2. Metaphorically, art therapy is similar to reading; there is the text and subtext. The reader relates to subtext as well as the text itself. As within the drawing, there is a text and a subtext; sometimes, the subtext can be revealed through the colors, the size and the interplay between the symbols.
3. Drawings should be viewed from all angles. You can see examples in some of Ziv's drawings; only after the drawing was turned upside-down, could Ziv understand the meaning of what she drew and the hidden issues. She drew unconsciously or unintentionally.
4. Drawing enables usage of all the senses, except taste, which were activated during the sexual abuse. The client touches (connecting with the canvas and the colors), sees (colors and symbols on the canvas), smells (the colors on the canvas), and hears (through the dialogue and narrative with the therapist). Thus, the drawings and the creation itself become a correctional experience for the sexual abuse.

In summary, in the case study, one can see that the use of drawings throughout the therapeutic process provided Ziv with continuity and depth. It encouraged and facilitated verbal communication and served as a catalyst to insights.

References

Bartholomew, K. (1990). Avoidance of intimacy: An attachment perspective. *Journal of Social and Personal Relationships, 7*, 147-178.

Bendall, S., Jackson, H., Hulbert, C. A., & McGorry, P. D. (2011). Childhood trauma and psychosis. *Family Matters, 89*, 53-60.

Banyard, V. L., Williams, L. M., & Siegel, J. A. (2001). Understanding links among childhood trauma, dissociation, and women's mental health. *American Journal of Orthopsychiatry, 71*(3), 311-321.

Bendall, S., Jackson, H., Hulbert, C.A., & McGorry, P.D. (2011). Childhood trauma and psychosis. *Family Matters, 89*, 53-60.

Bridges, M. R. (2006). Activating the corrective emotional experience. *Journal of Clinical Psychology, 62*, 551-568.

Briere, J. (1992). *Child Abuse Trauma: Theory and Treatment of the Lasting Effects.* London, UK: Sage Publications.

Briere, J., & Elliott, D. M. (1997). Psychological assessment of interpersonal victimization effects in adults and children. *Psychotherapy: Theory, Research & Practice, 34*, 353-364.

Burks, D., & Robbins, R. (2012). Psychologists'sauthenticity implications for work in professional and therapeutic settings. *Journal of Humanistic Psychology, 52* (1), 75-104.

Butler, W. M. (1999). Psychoanalytic time: A developmental perspective. *Canadian Journal of Psychoanalysis, 7*, 303-319.

Canton-Cortes, D. & Canton, J. (2010). Coping with child sexual abuse among college students and post-traumatic stress disorder: The role of continuity of abuse and relationship with the perpetrator. *Child Abuse and Neglect, 34*, 496-506.

Carlson, E. B., Ruzek, J. (2005). Effects of traumatic experiences: A national center for PTSD fact sheet. *National Center for Post-Traumatic Stress Disorder.* Archived from the original on 2004-06-12. Retrieved 2005-12-09.

Carstensen, L. (2006). The influence of a sense of time on human development. *Science*, 312, 1913-1915.

Chu, J. R. (1998). *Rebuilding shuttered lives: The responsible treatment of complex posttraumatic and dissociative disorders.* New York, NY: John Wiley & Sons.

Courtois, C. A. (1999). *Recollections of sexual abuse: Treatment principles and guidelines.* New York, NY: W. W. Norton & Co.

Crowder, C., & Lowe, P. (2000, May 19). Four accused in 'rebirthing' death.
Rocky Mountain News. Retrieved from http://www.rockymountainnews.com/drmn/local/article/0,1299,DRMN_15_691691,00.html

Crowely, S. (2000). *The search for autonomous intimacy: Sexual abuse and young women's identity development,* New York, NY: Peter Lang.

Cutajar, M. C., Mullen, P. E., Ogloff, J. R., Thomas, S. D., Wells, D. L., & Spataro, J. (2010). Psychopathology in a large cohort of sexually abused children followed up to 43 years. *Child Abuse and Neglect*, 34, 813-822.

D'Andrea, W., Ford, J., Stolbach, B., Spinazzola, J. & Van der Kolk, B. A. (2012). Understanding interpersonal trauma in children: Why we need a developmentally appropriate trauma diagnosis. *American Journal of Orthopsychiatry*, 82(2), 187-200.

DePrince, A. P., Brown, L. S., Cheit, R. E., Freyd, J. J., Gold, S. N., Pezdek, K., & Quina, K. (2012). Motivated forgetting and misremembering: Perspectives from betrayal trauma theory. *Nebraska Symposium on Motivation*, 58, 193-242.

Descutner, C. J., & Thelen, M. H. (1991). Development and validation of a fear-of-intimacy scale. *Journal of Consulting and Clinical Psychology*, 3(2), 218-225.

Downey, L. (2001). Intimacy and the relational self. *The Australian and New Zealand Journal of Family Therapy*, 22(3), 129-136.

Drake, L., Duncan, E., & Sutherland, F., Abernethy, C., & Henry, C. (2008). Time perspective and correlates of well-being. *Time & Society*, 17 (1), 47-61.

Eckhart, T. (1999). *The power of now.* Novato, CA: New World Library.

Ferguson, C. J., Rueda, S., Cruz, A., Ferguson, D., Fritz, S., & Smith, S. (2008). Violent video games and aggression: Causal relationship or byproduct of family violence and intrinsic violence motivation? *Criminal Justice and Behavior,* 35, 311-332.

Finkelhor, D., & Browne, A. (1985). The traumatic impact of child sexual abuse: A conceptualization. *American Journal of Orthopsychiatry,* 55(4), 530-541.

Firestone, R. W., & Catlett, J. (1999). *Fear of intimacy.* New York, NY: American Psychological Association.

Freud, A. (1936). *The ego and the mechanisms of defense.* London, UK: Hogarth Press.

Goleman, D. (1989, January 24). The sad legacy of abuse: A search for remedies. *New York Times.* Retrieved from http://www.nytimes.com/1989/01/24/science/sad-legacy-of-abuse-the-search-for-remedies.html?pagewanted=all&src=pm

Freyd, J. J. (1994). Betrayal trauma: Traumatic amnesia as an adaptive response to childhood abuse. *Ethics & Behavior,* 4, 307-329.

Freyd, J. J. (1996). *Betrayal trauma: The logic of forgetting childhood abuse.* Cambridge, MA: Harvard University Press.

Hall, E. T. (1966). *The Hidden Dimension.* New York, NY: Anchor Books.

Hammond, N. G. L., & Scullard, H. H. (1970). The Oxford Classical Dictionary 2nd Ed. Oxford, UK: Clarendon Press.

Hartman, D. & Zimberoff, D. (2004). Corrective emotional experience in the therapeutic process. *Journal of Heart-Centered Therapies,* 7(2), 3-84.

Hensley, A. L. (2009c). Betrayal trauma: Insidious purveyor of PTSD. In G. Dougherty (Ed.). *Return to equilibrium: Proceedings of the 7th Rocky Mountain Region Disaster Mental Health Conference* (pp. 105-148). Ann Arbor, MI: Loving Healing Press.

Hindess, B. (1972). The phenomenological sociology of Alfred Schutz. *Economy & Society,* 1(1), 1-27.

Hirsch, M. (1996). 2 forms of identification with the aggressor--according to Ferenczi and Anna Freud. *Prax Kinderpsychol Kinderpsychiatr.* 45(6), 198-205. [Article in German].

Jonas, S., Bebbington, McManus, S., Meltzer, H., Jenkins, R., Kuipers, E., Cooper, C., King, M., & Brugha, T. (2011). Sexual abuse and psychiatric disorder in England: results from the 2007 Adult Psychiatric Morbidity Survey Psychological Medicine. *Psychological Medicine,* 41(04), 709-719.

Jennings, A. G., & Armsworth, M. W. (1992). Ego development in women with histories of sexual abuse. *Child Abuse and Neglect,* 16(4), 553-565.

Kauffman, D. & Husman, J. (2004). Effects of time perspective on student motivation: Introduction to a special issue. *Educational Psychology Review,* 16, 1-7.

Kaufman, J.,& Zigler, E. (1989). The intergenerational transmission of child abuse (pp. 129-150), In D. Cicchetti & V. Carlson (Eds.), *Child maltreatment: Theory and research on the causes and consequences of child abuse and neglect.* Cambridge, UK: Cambridge University Press.

Kennedy, D. P., Glascher, J., Tyszka, J. M., & Adolphs, R. (2009). Personal space regulation by the human amygdala. *Natural Neuroscience,* 12, 1226-1227.

Krug, E. (2002). *World report on violence and health.* Geneva, Switzerland: World Health Organization.

Laaksonen, T., Sariola, H., Johansson, A., Jern, P., Varjonen, M., von der Pahlen, B., Sandnabba, N. K., & Santtila, P. (2011). Changes in the prevalence of child sexual abuse, its risk factors, and their associations as a function of age cohort in a Finnish population sample. *Child Abuse and Neglect,* 35(7), 480-90.

Lalor, K., & McElvaney R. (2010). Child sexual abuse, links to later sexual exploitation/high-risk sexual behavior, and prevention/treatment programs. *Trauma Violence Abuse,* 11(4), 159-77.

Lev-Wiesel, R., Amir, M. & Besser, A. (2005). Posttraumatic growth among female survivors of childhood sexual abuse in relation to the perpetrator identity. *Journal of Loss and Trauma,* 10(1), 7-17.

Levy, M. S. (1998). A helpful way to conceptualize and understand reenactments. *Journal of Psychotherapy Practice Research,* 7(3), 227-235.

Minkowski, E. (1933 Reedit 1955). *Le temps ve'cu.* Paris, France: P.U.F.

O'Leary, P., & Gould, N. (2009). 'Men who were sexually abused in childhood and subsequent suicidal ideation: Community comparison explanations and practice implications', *British Journal of Social Work,* 39, 950-968.

Ogden, C. K. (1928). *Plato theory of ethics*. London, UK: Routledge & Kegan Paul Ltd.

Pielage, B. S., Luteijn, F., & Arrindell, A. W. (2005). Adult attachment, intimacy and psychological distress in a clinical and community sample. *Clinical Psychology and Psychotherapy*, 12, 455-464.

Polusny, M. A., & Follette, V. M. (1995). Long-term correlates of child sexual abuse: Theory and review of empirical literature. *Applied and Preventive Psychology*, 4, 143-166.

Putnam, F. (1993). Dissociative disorders in children: Behavioral profiles and problems. *Child Abuse and Neglect*, 17(1), 39-45.

Rind, B., & Tromovitch, P. (1997). A meta-analytic review of findings from national samples on psychological correlates of child sexual abuse. *Journal of Sex Research*, 34 (3), 237.

Roth, S., Newman, E., Pelcovitz, D., van Der Kolk, B., & Mandel, F. S. (1997). Complex PTSD in victims exposed to sexual and physical abuse: Results from the DSM-IV field trial for Posttraumatic Stress Disorder. *Journal of traumatic stress*, 10(4), 539-555.

Russell, D. E. H. (1986). *The secret trauma: Incest in the lives of girls and women*. New York, NY: Basic Books.

Salter, D., McMillan, D., Richards, M., Talbot, T., Hodges, J., Bentovim, A., Hastings, R., Stevenson, J., & Skuse, D. (2003). Development of sexually abusive behavior in sexually victimized males: A longitudinal study. *Lancet*, 361(9356), 471-476.

Schalinski, I., Elbert, T., & Schauer, M. (2011). Female dissociative responding to extreme sexual violence in a chronic crisis setting: The case of Eastern Congo. *Journal of Trauma Stress*, 24(2), 235-8.

Seidman, B. T., Marshall, W. L., Hudson, S. M., & Robertson, P. J. (1994). An examination of intimacy and loneliness in sex offenders. *Journal of Interpersonal Violence*, 9, 518-534.

Urbach, G. (1979). The flavour of milk fat. In Proceedings of Milk Fat Symposium held at dairy research laboratory, Division of Food Research, CSIRO, 10th October, 1979, *Australian Society of Dairy Technology*, Melbourne, pp. 18-27.

van der Kolk, B. A., & van der Hart, O. (1989). Pierre Janet and the breakdown of adaptation in psychological trauma. *American Journal of Psychiatry*, 146, 1530-1540.

van der Kolk, B. A., & Greenberg, M. S. (1987).The psychobiology of the trauma response: Hyperarousal, constriction, and addiction to traumatic re-exposure. In B. A. van der Kolk (Ed.), *Psychological trauma* (pp.63-87). Washington, DC: American Psychiatric Press.

van der Kolk, B. A., & McFarlane, A. C. (1996). The black hole of trauma In B. A. van der Kolk, A. C. McFarlane, & L. Weisaeth, L. (Eds.), *Traumatic stress: The effects of overwhelming experience on mind, body, and society* (pp. 3-23). New York, NY: Guilford.

Volpicelli, J., Balaraman, G., Hahn, J., Wallace, H., Bux, D. (1999). The role of uncontrollable trauma in the development of PTSD and alcohol addiction. *Alcohol Research and Health,* 25(4), 256-261.

Weinberg, S. K. (1955). *Incest behaviour.* New York, NY: Citadel.

Whealin, J. (2004). *Child Sexual Abuse*, A National Center for PTSD Fact Sheet, Retrieved from www.ncptsd.org/facts/specific/fs_child_sexual_abuse.html, accessed October 27.

Windle, M., Windle, R. C., Scheidt, D. M., & Miller, G. B. (1995). Physical and sexual abuse and associated mental disorders among alcoholic inpatients. *American Journal of Psychiatry,* 152, 1322-1328.

Zimbardo, P. G. & Boyd, J. N. (1999) Putting time in perspective: A valid, reliable individual-differences metric. *Journal of Personality and Social Psychology,* 77(6), 1277-1288.

Acknowledgements

We would like to thank Elisheva Ackerson and Pora Kuperman for translating the original, Hebrew version of this book into English. We also would like to thank Lorisa Hasenbush and Elisheva Ackerson for their help in editing this English version.

www.ingramcontent.com/pod-product-compliance
Lightning Source LLC
Chambersburg PA
CBHW040457240426
43665CB00039B/72